MARC BERNARD

Translated by Jean M. Leblon

Zola

Evergreen Profile Book 16

GROVE PRESS, INC.   EVERGREEN BOOKS LTD.
NEW YORK   LONDON

First Published in This Edition 1960. All Rights Reserved.
Library of Congress Catalog Card Number: 60-7122
*Evergreen Profile Books are published
in the United States by Grove Press, Inc.
64 University Place   New York 3, N.Y.
in Great Britain by Evergreen Books Ltd.
20 New Bond Street   London, W. 1*
Distributed in Canada by McClelland & Stewart Ltd., 25 Hollinger Rd., Toronto 16
First published in France by Editions du Seuil, Paris, as Zola par lui-même
MANUFACTURED BY MOUTON & CO., IN THE NETHERLANDS

Zola
by Marc Bernard

Contents

- 5 Until the Age of Eighteen
- 11 The First Years in Paris
- 17 Publicity Chief
- 27 From 1866 to the War
- 35 Creation of the Rougon-Macquart
- 47 The Dram-shop
- 65 A Love Episode
- 71 Nana
- 91 The Ladies' Paradise
- 99 Germinal
- 117 The End of the Rougon-Macquart
- 135 The Dreyfus Case
- 151 Death
- 155 Zola: Simple and Complex
- 167 Zola After Death
- 178 *Opinions*
- 182 *Chronology*
- 183 *Bibliography*

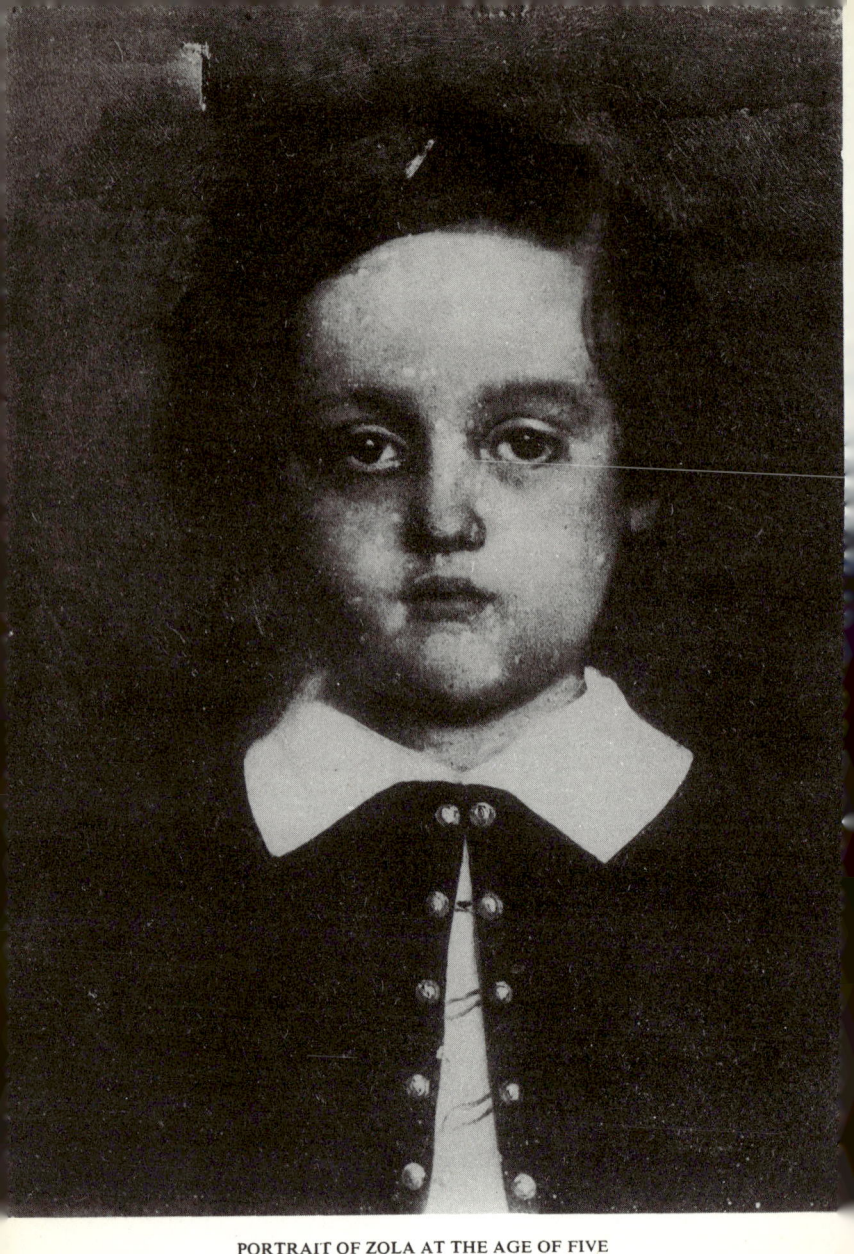

PORTRAIT OF ZOLA AT THE AGE OF FIVE

Is it possible to be so devoid of
doubt as to believe in oneself?
                    ZOLA

Until the Age of Eighteen, at Aix

Émile Zola was born in Paris, April 12, 1840. His mother was a Burgundian, and his father Italian. François Zola, an engineer, lived in Aix-en-Provence where he was engaged in the construction of a canal which was to be given his name.

During a stay in Paris where he had gone to obtain the help necessary for the realization of his project, he had met a young lady of nineteen, Émilie-Aurélie Aubert. François Zola was forty-three; a man of quick determination, he decided to marry the girl as soon as he laid eyes on her.

It was during another one of his parents' stays in Paris that Émile was born in the apartment which his father had rented at 10 rue Saint-Joseph, very near the rue Montmartre.

After he had concluded his business, François Zola returned to Aix with his wife and son. He died there in 1847.

Émile Zola is seven years old when his father dies. Until the age of twelve, he goes to boarding school at Notre-Dame, then to the *collège* of Aix. He is a member of the band and plays the clarinet in the processions, between chapters of a novel he has begun about the Crusades. After a mediocre beginning he suddenly applies himself to his work, and he finishes in first place in most of the examinations at the end of the school year.

Bonne maman,

Loin de toi je pense à ta fête que je ne puis te souhaiter de vive voix, ce jour sera pour moi un motif de plus pour me donner un souvenir de tous les bons soins dont tu as entouré mon jeune âge, reçois ici l'expression des vœux de ton petit fils, qui sont de te voir heureuse et jouir dans tes vieux jours d'une tranquillité parfaite, je ferai tout ce qui dépendra de moi pour contribuer à ton bonheur et te servir d'appui aussi longue que mon âge le permettra.

Un souvenir est tout ce que je t'envoie, je ne possède rien que je puisse t'offrir, à mon retour près de toi si je ne suis pas plus riche je pourrai que te dire: bonne maman voici ton petit fils et le renouvelle ses vives affections, d'ici je te vois sourire en bonne mère et ton cœur, j'en suis sûr, répond à l'avance que c'est tout ce qu'il veut.

Je prie ma cousine de t'embrasser, plus

SEPTIÈME.

DEUXIÈME DIVISION.
M. SILVESTRE, *professeur.*

EXCELLENCE.
Prix.

1ᵉʳ RIMBAUD Onésime, de Grimaud (Var), int.
2ᵉ LAFAYE René, d'Aix, ext.

Accessit.

1ᵉʳ ZOLA Emile, de Paris, 2 f. n.
2ᵉ BEDARRIDE Lucien d'Aix, ext.

THÈME.
Prix.

1ᵉʳ RIMBAUD Onésime, int., 2 f. n.
2ᵉ ZOLA Emile, int., 3 f. n.

Accessit.

1ᵉʳ BEDARRIDE Lucien, ext., **2** f. n.
2ᵉ LAFAYE René, ext., **2** f. n.

VERSION.
Prix.

1ᵉʳ ZOLA Emile, int., 4 f. n.
2ᵉ RIMBAUD Onésime, int. 3 f. n.

Accessit.

1ᵉʳ BEDARRIDE Lucien, ext., 3 f. n.
2ᵉ LEMATICOT Paul, de Lorient, ext.

GRAMMAIRE FRANÇAISE ET CALCUL.
Prix.

1ᵉʳ BEDARRIDE Lucien, ext., 4 f. n.
2ᵉ RIMBAUD Onésime, int., 4 f. n.

Accessit.

1ᵉʳ LEMATICOT Paul, ex., 2 f. n.
2ᵉ ZOLA Emile, int., 5 f. n.

HISTOIRE ET GÉOGRAPHIE.
Prix.

1ᵉʳ ZOLA Emile, int., 6 f. n.
2ᵉ LAFAYE René, ext., 3 f. n.

Accessit.

1ᵉʳ RIMBAUD Onésime, int., 5 f. n.
2ᵉ CHIRIS Antoine, de Riez (Var), int.

RÉCITATION CLASSIQUE.
Prix.

1ᵉʳ ZOLA Emile, int., 7 f. n.
2ᵉ RIMBAUD Onésime, int., 6 f. n.

To his grandmother,
July 12, 1851

Honors list at the Collège
of Aix (August 10, 1853)

Although his ties with Provence are casual, the impressions of his childhood and adolescence will be lasting ones. He will in no way be a regional writer, he will not be faithful to Provence in the way Paul Arène or Alphonse Daudet have been, but he will always remember his walks in the country around Aix with Cézanne and Baille, and he will always speak of that period of his life with some emotion; there are, as a matter of fact, many people from Provence in his writings, and he will remain faithful to the friends of his early years.

The southern landscapes made a vivid impression on him; they appear frequently in his books.

The Paradou will remain for him a kind of oasis, a true paradise. He knows well the heath around Aix, from the long walks he has taken there with his school friends; he has swum in the Arc, cooked his meals on fires of dried grass, explored caves, and his wanderings have given him such a taste for freedom that the memories of that period sometimes will bring tears to his eyes. A customs clerk at twenty, he will let his imagination escape from his drab little office to the Aix countryside.

His taste for literature has grown in the open air rather than in the classroom, in the shadow of the sycamores, while he recited passages from *Jocelyn* or *Hernani*. His favorite writers at this point are Lamartine, Hugo, and Musset. Cézanne and he are wild romantics; between swims, Ruy Blas and Don Salluste are heard.

Pp. 9-10. A last glance at his father's work (the François Zola canal and dam), and at the countryside which Émile leaves at eighteen

The First Years in Paris

After François Zola's death in 1847, the household deteriorated gradually from poverty to near misery, until Madame Zola, eleven years later, was forced to leave Aix and to go to Paris to live. At this time Émile is eighteen; he attends the *lycée* Saint-Louis, where Henri de Rochefort and the future General de Gallifet are also enrolled. Because of his accent, his schoolmates call him the *Marseillais*. He is studying for a baccalaureate in sciences, but he fails and goes to spend his vacation at Aix. He tries again in November of the same year, 1859, this time in Marseille, preferring to try his luck with provincial examiners. Again no luck, and, again *because of his French*.... Madame Zola is discouraged; she can no longer afford to leave her son at the *lycée*; he will have to get a job. A friend of the family will find him one in the Customs Department at the Napoleon Docks. He will earn sixty francs a month and despair at the thought of the commonplace life awaiting him.

Since he knows no one in Paris, he writes long letters to his friends in Aix. In one of his first letters to Baille, dated January 23, 1859, he tells him of his need to earn a living; it is a problem which will torment him for many years.

I told you in my last letter of my intention to get a clerical job as soon as possible; it was a desperate and absurd resolution. My future was ruined, I was destined to rot on a rush-bottomed chair, to moulder, to get in a rut and stay there. I could foresee these sad consequences, and I felt the instinctive shiver that precedes a plunge into cold water. Fortunately I was held back at the brink of the precipice; my eyes were opened, and I drew back in horror at the thought of such abysmal depths, of the mud and the rocks waiting for me at the bottom. None of that office life! None of that sewer!, I cried. Then I looked all around, screaming for advice. . . .

But it was hunger which gave him the strongest advice:

My mother still supports me, and she can hardly take care of herself. I must look for work in order to eat, and although I have not found it yet, I hope to have work soon. Such then is my situation; to earn my bread any way I can, and, if I cannot forego my dreams, busy myself at night with my future. The struggle will be a long one, but it does not frighten me; I feel something inside of me, which, if it exists, will sooner or later come out in the broad daylight.

And Zola discovers that it is not so easy to earn his bread, even if it is "any way he can":

I should like to be able to give you some assurance concerning my material situation. Unfortunately, nothing is less sure than that part of my future. For more than a year I have furiously hunted for possibilities; but if I run well, they run away even better. I have made application after application; I have gone to all kinds of offices: long waits everywhere, with never any result. . . . You would not believe how difficult it is for me to find a job. And it is not because I set any conditions, nor that I want to do certain things rather than others; in the beginning I had that kind of pride, today it is all gone!

Finally in April of 1860, he is a customs clerk at sixty francs a month. That, of course, is not very exciting. Émile says so to Baille, not without some bitterness:

As for my life, it is still monotonous. Hunched over my desk I write without knowing what I am writing, and I sleep

> awake, in a daze. Sometimes, all of a sudden, a bright recollection comes to my mind, one of our gay parties, or one of the spots we loved so well, and my heart grows heavy. I look up and I see the sad reality; the dusty room, littered with old papers, filled with a crowd of clerks most of whom are stupid; I hear the monotonous scratching of the pens, the shrill words, the strange terms uttered around me; and there, on the window pane, as if to mock me, the rays of the sun come to play and to tell me that outdoors nature rejoices, that birds sing melodiously, and flowers fill the air with intoxicating perfumes. I lean back in my chair, close my eyes, and for a moment I see you going by, you, my friends; I can also see those women whom I loved without knowing it. Then it all fades away, reality comes back more terrifying than before, I take up my pen again, and I feel like weeping.

He will not be able to bear for long that "world of stupid clerks": two months later he resigns. A short new Bohemian period begins for him: he lives in his attic eating bread dipped in oil and rubbed with garlic.

During that whole first phase of his life in Paris, in spite of his failures as a student and the uncertainty of his future, Zola never lets himself be driven to discouragement. He still believes in that "something" inside him, and he is ready to fight in order to "bring it out in the broad daylight."

In December, 1859, he tells Baille that he has completed his first prose work:

> I do not see anyone, and the evenings seem long. I smoke a lot, I read a lot, and I write very little. However, I have finished *The Girls of Provence (Les Grisettes de Provence)*; I have had a certain pleasure in telling those foolish things. But I am far from satisfied with my work: the material was extremely difficult; events raced one after the other, there was no climax and no denouement. Moreover, it lacked dignity and morality; our roles were also far from being those of the heroes of novels. . . .

Such dissatisfaction does not break down the confidence which he has in himself: "It is not that my inspiration has waned; in my daydreams, my mind is as powerful as before, my ideas just as ambitious."

In the same letter to Baille, he outlines a creed to which he will remain faithful:

> To be unknown forever leads one to lose his trust in himself; nothing enlarges the thinking of an author like success. However, in order to become well-known, I must continue to work; I am young, and, if I have suffered from uneasiness and disillusion the last few months, all poetry in me cannot have been smothered.

The theme reappears many times during that period. In May, 1860:

> I told you in my last letter that for me, happiness would be found in great tranquillity, both around me and within me. Since this dream might seem to you to contradict my other dream of literary renown, I said that I would come back to that subject. You probably do not know the thoughts that come to my mind at the mention of the word "author."

Similarly, a little later these prophetic lines:

> As for the future, I do not know; if I definitely take up a literary career, I want to follow my motto: *All or nothing!* Consequently I do not wish to follow in anybody else's footsteps; not because I covet the title of master of a school – usually such a man is consistently systematic – but I should like to find an unexplored path, and to break out of the present crowd of scribblers.

That which he will achieve about ten years later – the creation of a team with Flaubert, the Goncourt brothers, Alphonse Daudet – he proposes now to Baille and Cézanne:

> The principal goal of this association would be to form a strong nucleus for the future, to help one another whatever position we may enjoy. We are young, the universe is ours; would it not be wise, before we rush ahead, to shake hands, to create a new bond between us so that once we are in the fight we may feel at our side a friend, that ray of hope in the human night.

What he does not know is what he will write later on. Baille is a realist, and Zola takes great pains to show him that such a conception of the world is false:

I used to be profoundly irritated by your stubborn refusal to understand my philosophy. It did not help me to cry out to you: "Reality is sad, reality is hideous; we must hide it under flowers; let us not deal with it any more than is demanded by our miserable human condition; let us eat, drink, satisfy all our brutal appetites, but let us leave our soul its due, may dreams embellish our hours of leisure." Invariably you answered that I was losing myself in the clouds, that I did not see what was before my eyes. Good God! – we must not see it. I turn my eyes away from the manure-heap and look at the roses; I do not deny the usefulness of the manure which helps my roses to bloom, but I prefer the roses, useless as they are. I react the same way to the real and the ideal. I accept the former as necessary, I subject myself to it according to nature; but, as soon as I can escape the vulgar rut, I run to the other and I lose myself in my meadows.

And as Baille does not let himself be converted very easily to the idealism of his friend, Zola comes back:

When we stir filth some stains always remain on our hands; when we amble in the fields at dawn, we always come back with the sweet scent of flowers and dew. The satirical poet always sees the worse side of man; first he pities man, then despises him, and finally hates him; his laughter, scornful at first, becomes bitter; the more he goes on, the deeper the mud gets, the harder, the more pitiless he becomes; his last word is blasphemy.

While pursuing his fight against realism, Zola changes his residence many times, never straying very far from the Panthéon where later . . .

I have moved, and my new address is 21 rue Neuve-Saint-Étienne-du-Mont. I live in a little attic with a fine view, formerly occupied by Bernardin de Saint-Pierre, and where, they say, he wrote most of his works. An auspicious garret for a poet.

Since he cannot afford to buy coal in the winter, he wraps himself up in a blanket: he calls it "making like an Arab." He dreams of the future; he writes bad poetry; he feels simple emotions:

For nearly two weeks now I have been spinning a most Platonic tale of love. A young lady, a flower-girl who lives next door to me, walks under my window twice a day, at six-thirty in the morning and eight at night. She is blond, dainty, and graceful; small hands, small feet, the prettiest little maid. Every time she is due to come by, I place myself at the window: she comes, looks up; we exchange a look, a smile even; and it is all over.

Bernardin de Saint-Pierre's garret has made a definite impression on his imagination; he sees in it more than a coincidence: it is an omen from the past. He says so to Cézanne:

I do not know really what fate guides me in the choice of my living quarters. While a small child in Aix I lived in Thiers' house. I come to Paris and my first room happens to have been Raspail's; then today, by some mysterious chance, I move away from that splendid eighth floor – about which I spoke to you last spring – and I happen to pick a new garret, the same where Bernardin de Saint-Pierre wrote most of his works. This new little room is a true jewel; small, I must admit, but sunny and above all most original. One climbs up to it by a spiral staircase; there are two windows, one to the south and one to the north. In a word, a little room with a view of practically the whole city. I almost forgot to tell you that my new street is called Neuve-Saint-Étienne-du-Mont and that my new number is 21.

Cézanne's and Baille's reactions are soon to disappoint him: one is slow, the other is always afraid of "falling into someone's clutches." When Zola indicates their roles to them, when he dreams of forming the team in which, one helping the other, they will reach the summit, they shy away, hang back, and refuse to share his grand visions.

From that time on, the principle traits of his character are clearly defined: passion for work, will, self-confidence, love of the struggle, and a certain dogmatism. This singularly active dreamer is a tall young man, near-sighted, with wide shoulders; stockily built, awkward, and with a speech defect that changes *s* into *f*.

Publicity Chief

In February, 1862, in order to make a living, but also to get closer to the literary world, Zola goes to work at Hachette's. His first job is to wrap packages. Here he is on the first step of the ladder that will lead him to glory; all he has to do is to climb. Without losing any time, he gets ready to do just that. Very soon he gets up to the second floor where he becomes publicity chief. It is not exactly what he was hoping for when he placed the manuscript of a poem on his boss' desk. The poem will not be published, but M. Hachette is interested and he gives his employee a raise. Émile now earns two hundred francs a month.

More truly profitable will be the experience which he is to gain while trying to sell the works of his fellow writers. His new functions put him in contact with some of the best-known writers of the day: Guizot, Lamartine, Michelet, Littré, Sainte-Beuve. Taine shows up often because readers write to him there to give him their suggestions about his *History of English Literature*. Others come too, even more assiduously: some of the more obscure novelists, such as Amédée Achard, de Lanoye, Francis Rey, and others who are famous, such as Edmond About.

Zola also discovers that writing is a trade, a business, and that the value of a literary work is not always enough to feed its writer without the help of publicity, cleverness, intrigues, and contacts. To be sure, Émile Zola suspected it, thanks to his flair for realism. He now finds himself among the writers whom he had admired from a distance, when he stood on the other side of the fence, lost in the crowd of readers; he hears their confidences, he sees their anxieties, listens to their complaints, learns from them the best ways of making a book sell. The lesson will not go unheeded.

Such discoveries do not disturb him. A book is supposed to be sold, and all means to that end are good. Émile Zola is delighted to find himself in this confessional. Each writer unmasks himself as he steps into it. Zola listens, acts, and remembers. The novelists who speak to him little dream that this young man of twenty-two will outshine them all, that the count of his books in print will reach numbers which they would never dare dream of, that his commercial as well as literary success will be one of the most astonishing of the century, and that he will become Hugo's direct rival. For the time being, the publicity chief sends statements to the newspapers extolling the merits of Amédée Achard's or Francis Rey's latest novel.

While trying to market the productions of the others, Zola is working at his own. He has probably noted the small number of books of poems sold, for he will write only prose from now on; he seeks consolation by polishing his style.

He has been a naturalized citizen since 1862, but the drawing of lots for conscription leaves him exempt from military duty. He can thus quietly employ his hours of leisure in the writing of his *Tales for Ninon* (*Contes à Ninon*) which he finishes at the age of twenty-four. Three editors refuse the manuscript, but Zola can no longer keep his works in a drawer; he is determined to find a door he can open.

When he enters M. Lacroix's office, he begins with these words: "Three editors have refused this manuscript." Lacroix looks with amazement at the young writer so eager to admit something which his fellow writers prefer to keep quiet. But the amazement is sympathetic. Zola, furthermore, adds immediately: "I have talent." He says it without arrogance, even with a little embarrassment, as if it were an obvious quality which it would be useless to conceal. His tone has such a quiet conviction that Lacroix is taken. And so is the manuscript.

ÉMILE ZOLA

CONTES A NINON

A Ninon.
Simplice. — Le Carnet de Danse.
Celle qui m'aime. — La Fée Amoureuse.
Le Sang. — Les Voleurs et l'Ane.
Sœur-des-Pauvres.
Aventures du grand Sidoine
et du petit Médéric.

PARIS
LIBRAIRIE INTERNATIONALE
15, BOULEVARD MONTMARTRE
au coin de la rue Vivienne
J. HETZEL ET A. LACROIX, ÉDITEURS

Tous droits de traduction et de reproduction réservés

All Zola has to do now is to act, for he is not one of those who wait for luck and fame to cross his threshold: he eagerly takes the first steps. Consequently, it is he who shows Lacroix the way to make people buy a book; and since there are some steps which an author cannot decently take himself, he suggests them.

His taste for glory, his desire to "arrive," has perhaps never been so neatly, so realistically asserted. The time for dreaming in attics is over; the public is there, it must be conquered.

Zola does not doubt for a moment that he will succeed; no hesitation nor false modesty; he knows exactly what he wants and how to get it.

Baille and Cézanne have come to Paris to join him. From now on (1864-1867), Zola's regular correspondent will be Antony Valabrègue who remains in Aix. The style of the letters has changed; it has become concise, hurried; it is pared of the adolescent ramblings. Somewhat coyly, Zola affects laziness:

> I am letting my pen run while I write you as if I were a man in a hurry, not because I have a lot to do at this time, but I am so lazy that I always hurry to finish what I have begun, in order to have nothing to do afterwards.

We can see that it is an unusual laziness, and it does not deceive Valabrègue, since Zola feels he must explain:

> I do not know whether you will believe me: I have not been able to answer you sooner for lack of time some days, for lack of gaiety other days. It would be easier, I know, to explain all this by a good siege of laziness. However, my industrious laziness, as you like to call my usual punctuality, has nothing to do with it in this case; I shall be, if you really want it, slothfully slothful.

When his friend blames him for having written an article too personal in character, Zola answers him: "Come now, do not fear to say 'I'; the day that your 'I' will become famous, it will be the 'I' of a whole crowd of people."

The motto of this Napoleon of literature is simple: "You know what I shouted to you from my threshold when you were already on the second floor: 'Produce, produce!' "

In the midst of everything he organizes the publicity for his book:

I have won my first victory. Hetzel has accepted my first book of stories; the volume will be published about the beginning of next October. The struggle was short, and I am amazed that I was not more bruised. I am on the threshold, the battlefield is wide, and I may still very well break my neck. It does not matter; since there is nothing left to do but go straight ahead, I shall go ahead. Get ready to write an article about me, it doesn't matter where; I want to give all of you the satisfaction of contradicting me.

But those insipid *Tales for Ninon,* which hardly foreshadow the subsequent astonishing power of the writer, invite little contradiction. A few weeks later, in a long letter to Valabrègue, Zola expounds already what he calls his "theory of Screens."

In a literary work we see the universe through a man, through a temperament, a personality. The picture which appears on this new kind of Screen is the reproduction of the things and the people standing beyond, and this reproduction, which cannot be faithful, will change as many times as a new Screen comes between our eye and the universe. Likewise, eyeglasses of different colors give different colors to the same objects; likewise, concave or convex lenses change the shape of objects, each in a different way.

That theory leads him to criticize in the following terms what he will do later himself: "Each school has this in it which is monstrous: it forces nature to lie according to certain rules."
As for realism, for which he criticized Baille so sharply four years earlier, he claims it for his own now, still judging it fairly objectively:

The realistic Screen is a mere piece of window glass, very thin, very clear, and pretending to be so perfectly transparent that the pictures go through it and are reproduced in all their reality. Thus, there are no changes in the lines nor in the colors: it is an exact reproduction, frank and naïve. The realistic Screen denies its own existence. Truly there is too much pride there. Whatever may be said of it, it does exist, and thus cannot boast of reproducing the universe in all the truth of its splendid beauty. However clear, however thin this pane be, it still has its own color, and a certain thickness; it does color objects and it refracts them just as does any other. However, I do admit willingly that the pictures it presents are the most real; it often achieves a high degree of exactness. It is certainly difficult to define a Screen that has for its principal quality that of hardly existing; I believe, however, it is accurate to say that a fine gray dust blurs its clarity. Any object that passes through it loses some of its brilliance, or rather it becomes slightly darker. On the other hand, lines become heavier, exaggerated so to speak in their width. Life spreads itself generously on the Screen; it is a gross and somewhat heavy life.

And here is the first stand taken by the future leader of the naturalistic school:

> If I must say it, the realistic Screen has all my sympathy; it satisfies my reason, and I sense in it immense beauties of strength and truth. However, I repeat that I cannot accept it in the way it is insistently presented to me; I cannot admit that it gives us true pictures; and I maintain that there must be in it some peculiar properties which deform the pictures and which, consequently, make works of art out of them. I fully accept the method, which consists of standing squarely in front of nature and reproducing it in its entirety without omission.

At the same time, Zola puts full determination into the pursuit of commercial success for his book:

> ... I am seeking for my book as much publicity as possible and I hope for a brilliant result. Thank God, it is almost all finished: the book is being bound, my letters of advice are written, my advertisement drawn up: I am waiting.

His schedule is not exactly that of a lazy man:

> You would not believe how busy I am; I have undertaken so much work that I do not know where to begin: first of all, I spend ten hours at the bookshop every day; then every week I hand in an article of 100 to 150 lines to the *Petit Journal*, and every other week an article of 500 to 600 lines to the *Salut public* of Lyon; finally I have my novel, on which I should work instead of letting it lie quietly at the bottom of a drawer. You understand that I do not write all that prose for love of the public; the *Petit Journal* pays me 20 francs per article, and the *Salut public* 50 to 60 francs; so that I make about 200 francs a month with my pen. The

17.

LIBRAIRIE
de
L. HACHETTE ET Cⁱᵉ
Rue Pierre Sarrazin, 14

Paris, 3 février 1865

Messieurs

Je suis chargé de faire, dans le Salut public, de Lyon, une Revue littéraire de quinzaine, et j'aurai le plus vif désir de consacrer un grand article à votre dernière œuvre, *Germinie Lacerteux*.

Auriez-vous l'extrême obligeance de me faire remettre ce volume ?

financial factor has influenced my decision in all this; still I consider journalism such a powerful lever that I am not at all unhappy to be able to appear at regular intervals before a considerable number of readers. That thought should explain to you my joining the staff of the *Petit Journal*. I do not know how that sheet rates in the literary field, but I do know that its writers enjoy a quick popularity.

For fear that Valabrègue may still not understand the meaning of his efforts, he summarizes thus: "Right now I have two aims, one is to make myself well-known, the other to increase my revenue. May Heaven help me!"

Still he prefers not to rely too much on help from heaven, so he adopts the following method of work, which he will follow to the end:

Now I must forge ahead, forge ahead at all costs. Good or bad, the written page must be published. Altogether, the thought of emerging out of the crowd excites in me an actual sensual pleasure, and I feel certain anguish when I ask myself whether I shall have the necessary strength, whether I shall be able to maintain myself on the step of the ladder that I shall have reached.

Valabrègue's provincialism helps him retain some illusions regarding the intrinsic value of the written word. Zola brings him bluntly back to reality:

If you only knew, my poor friend, how little talent counts in the search for success, you would abandon pen and paper and you would set out to analyze the ways of the literary world, the thousand little tricks that open doors, the art of using other people's credit, the cruelty which is necessary to run over the dear fellow-writers.

Over and over again the theme reappears:

Do you really understand me, are you listening? We are impatient people, we demand rapid success – why not admit it? – we must thus make our own success. Noises fade out, talent remains. I realize that indifference would be loftier and nobler; but, as I have told you, we are the children of an impatient age, we are furiously eager to raise ourselves higher and higher, and if we do not trample on the others, rest assured that they will trample us underfoot.

Since the death of François Zola, Madame Zola and her son have had nothing but difficulties with the city of Aix. Valabrègue has just informed his friend that the municipal authorities want to change the name of the Zola canal.

You tell me that they are in the process of removing the name of Zola from the canal which my father built. Please give me more details in your next letter: tell me how and in what circumstances the change of name has been attempted. You must understand that particularly at this moment I hardly care about the weak renown that a name on a wall can afford me; as for me, I feel strong enough to build several walls. But I have a duty to fulfill, and if I should write a letter, I shall write it, even if only to protest.

And Zola, dreaming of another glory, ends in this fashion: "Take heart, my dear Valabrègue, I have much hope. We are young, and there are many fortresses to conquer."

From now on he will never stop; death alone will put an end to his activity. He will write a novel a year, often in two volumes, not to mention the plays and critical works, and the countless articles.

From 1866 to the War

The *Tales for Ninon* appeared in 1864, *Claude's Confession (La Confession de Claude)* in 1865; the two books were fairly well received by the critics. As a result, on the eighth of January, 1866, Zola announces his momentous decision to his friend Valabrègue: he will leave the Hachette firm, and he will devote himself entirely to his writing. For the first time he expresses his often ill-fated passion for the theater:

> I am leaving the firm at the end of January; I shall replace the office work by the work I shall do on some books that were ordered from me while I was at Hachette's. I shall get busy with the theater; all the editors will now open their doors to me; but I have more than one string to my bow; I shall have to attack from the side most favorable to profit and fame. Moreover, I plan to write more or less regularly in two or three newspapers. I shall coin as much money as possible. Besides, I have faith in myself, and I am vigorously and merrily going ahead.

It does not take him long, however, to realize that he has deceived himself, that he is not made to compete with the precisionists of prose, and that he is wasting his time struggling for the grace of a Musset or a Gautier; a more strenuous task awaits him. He is tempted by realism; he has drawn closer to it, rather shyly still, in *Claude's Confession*. *Thérèse Raquin*, four years after the publication of the *Tales for Ninon*, marks a definite step. He is twenty-eight.

What he needs henceforth is a slice of life, rare if possible. Turning his back on Musset, he shuns the romanticism which he loved so well in his adolescent years. His masters are Balzac, Stendhal, Duranty, Flaubert. The realism which heretofore horrified him will be his daily bread. But he mixes a few spices in it. Like the ogre, he demands the whole man. What an appetite, and what impatience!

While he is working on *Thérèse Raquin*, someone suggests to him that he write a huge serial novel about the mysterious events in Marseille. He tells Valabrègue about it in a letter dated February 19, 1867:

> You must have heard that I am going to undertake a large work in the *Messager de Provence*, a Marseille newspaper; I am to publish in it a long novel, beginning March 1; it will be called *The Mysteries of Marseille (Les Mystères de Marseille)*, and it is based on the documents of the recent criminal trials. I am swamped with papers; I do not know how I shall bring an orderly world out of this chaos. It is a poorly paid job, but I expect a great reaction in the south. It is not bad to get a whole section of the country on your side. Besides, I have accepted the propositions made to me because I am as always driven by that spirit of work and struggle of which I have spoken to you earlier. I like difficulties, impossibilities. Especially I like life, and I believe that it is always preferable to produce anything than to lie idle. Thanks to such beliefs I shall be able to accept all the challenges that will be offered to me in my fight against myself or against the public. I am told that the announcement of *The Mysteries of Marseille* has made a certain impression down there. Circulars will be distributed, and posters hung. If you ever hear anything special about my novel, please let me know.

To Valabrègue who has blamed him for accepting a task which is unworthy of his talent, Zola answers:

> I need the public, I approach it as best I can, I try every way I know to tame it. For the time being I need two things above all others: publicity and money.

ÉMILE ZOLA

LES MYSTÈRES
DE
MARSEILLE

ROMAN HISTORIQUE CONTEMPORAIN

PREMIÈRE PARTIE.

MARSEILLE
IMP. NOUVELLE A. ARNAUD, RUE VACON, 21.
—
1867.

Les cadavres restèrent toute la nuit sur le carreau de la salle à manger, tordus, vautrés, éclairés de lueurs jaunâtres par les clartés de la lampe que l'abat-jour jetait sur eux. Et pendant plus de douze heures, jusqu'au lendemain vers midi, Mme Raquin, roide et muette, les contempla à ses pieds, ne pouvant rassasier ses yeux, les écrasant de regards lourds.

EMILE ZOLA.

Last page of a pre-publication copy of *Thérèse Raquin*, under the title "A Marriage of Love"

Nonetheless he has no illusions about the quality of his serial. The only thing he holds dear is *Thérèse Raquin,* and he calls the book his "great psychological and physiological study."

> I speak to you as a friend. It is understood that I concede what you say about *The Mysteries of Marseille.* I know what I am doing. At the moment, I am working on three novels at the same time: *The Mysteries,* a short novel for *L'Illustration,* and a large psychological study for *La Revue du XIXe Siècle.* I am very happy with the latter; it is, I believe, the best thing I have done so far. I am even afraid that it might be too strong, and that Houssaye will balk at the last moment. It will appear in three parts; the first part is finished and is due to be published in May. You see that I don't waste any time. Last month I wrote that first part – a third of the volume – as well as about a hundred pages of the *Mysteries.* I am hunched over my desk from morning till night.

On May 29, 1867, he speaks about it again to Valabrègue:

> I am very happy with the psychological and physiological novel which I am going to publish in *La Revue du XIXe Siècle.* It is almost completed and it will surely be my best work. I believe that I put all my heart and body into it. I am even afraid that I put a little too much of my body in it and that I shall offend the Attorney General. However, a few months in prison do not frighten me.

His friend is not the only one who hears such open confessions; one of Zola's qualities is frankness. When he presents some articles to Alphonse Duchesne, M. de Villemessant's collaborator on the *Figaro,* on April 11, 1865, he writes as plainly as he does in his letters to Valabrègue:

> Permit me to introduce myself, since nobody has recommended me, and since I prefer not to incur your distrust by any kind of patronage.
>
> I have recently published a collection of short stories which has had a certain amount of success, I write a literary column in the *Salut public,* and I send articles to the *Petit Journal.* Such is my output.
>
> I wish to increase my production and to succeed as soon as possible. I thought of your newspaper as the one which, in my haste, can bring me renown the fastest. I come to you

À Monsieur le Maire, et à messieurs les
membres du Conseil Municipal de la Ville d'Aix

Messieurs

Je viens de recevoir une ampliation de votre
délibération du 6 novembre 1868 et du décret
du 19 décembre suivant, qui ont
décidé, à la suite de la demande que j'avais eu
l'honneur de vous adresser, de donner au boulevard du Chemin Neuf la dénomination de
Boulevard François Zola, en reconnaissance
des services rendus à votre cité par mon
père.

Je m'empresse, messieurs, de vous té-
moigner toute ma gratitude. Je savais que
je ne me rappellerais pas les travaux de mon
père, sans que votre générosité ne s'émût
des retards mis à récompenser la mémoire d'un homme
qui s'est devoué aux intérêts des citoyens
que vous représentez si dignement. Mais
malgré la certitude que j'avais de ne
pas m'adresser inutilement à vos co...
j'ai été profondément touché de l'unani...

First draft of a letter in which Zola thanks the Municipal Council of Aix whic

avec laquelle vous avez bien voulu votre ...
recompense civique à l'ingénieur français
Zola. Je sais maintenant que ma démarche
était le vœu de tous.

Veuillez croire à ma reconnaissance profonde.
Si je ne suis pas un fils de votre ville, j'ai
grandi à Aix et je me considère un
peu comme son enfant d'adoption. Aujourd'hui,
un nouveau lien m'attache fortement à elle.

Je vous prie, messieurs, de vouloir bien
agréer l'assurance de mes sentiments les plus
distingués et les plus respectueux.

at his request, has just named one of the city's boulevards after his father.

> candidly; I am sending you a few pages of my prose and I ask you in all simplicity: Does it suit you? If my limited personality displeases you, let us forget the whole thing; if it is only the enclosed article that you do not like, I can write some others.
>
> I am young and, I must admit, I have faith in myself. I know that you like to try people out, to create new writers. Do try me out and create me. You will always have the pick of the crop.

It is not long before such an attitude and such efforts bear fruit. Émile Zola, who has just married, can finally move into a real apartment. He announces it, full of pride, to his friend Coste in a letter of July 26, 1866:

> I do not live in the rue de L'École-de-Médecine any more. My wife and I now live at 10 rue de Vaugirard, next to the Odéon. We have a full apartment with a dining room, a bedroom, a living room, a kitchen, a guest-room and a terrace. It is a veritable palace; we shall open its doors wide when you return.

But it would be wrong to say that he "settles down" morally speaking, and that he is going to rest on his early laurels: "In short I am satisfied with my accomplishments so far. But I have an impatient nature, and I should like to go even faster."

However great his impatience, Zola will be forced to slow down for a while. Although the publication of *Thérèse Raquin* has attracted the attention of the critics, the wide public which he seeks so obstinately still remains to be heard from. And the publication during the following year of *Madeleine Férat* does not improve the novelist's situation very much.

Writing *The Mysteries of Marseille* has taught him his craft and a method. From the mass of documents which he acquired, he extracted stories which he organized around a central theme: he will use the same method for the *Rougon-Macquart* series; again, before each new novel he will assemble all kinds of notes and information about the milieu which he is to describe. The writing of that serial also taught him to abandon the pursuit of style, which does not suit him; furthermore, he now understands that the perfection in details must be sacrificed to the overall effect, to the value of the whole. Nevertheless, though his technique is perfected, Zola seems to be a powerful machine still idling.

Creation of the Rougon-Macquart

Going from novel to unrelated novel, starting anew each time with a new story, is still not what really suits Zola's talent. It is as if he could not bring himself to broaden his scope.

Balzac's example tempts him, however; he admires Balzac more than any other writer. He should really like to create his own *Human Comedy,* but he does not know how to go about it. To be sure, the model is there, but it is still beyond his reach. Zola waits for the time when he can seize it, make it his own. He does not dare touch it, perhaps for fear of being accused of slavish imitation. His inspiration will come from science – which had tempted Zola earlier when he was a student a few years before. He catches himself dreaming of a synthesis which would make a literary work out of a scientific one, and would thus conciliate his two leanings and enable him to pursue the two vocations which he feels inside himself.

Claude Bernard's *Introduction to the Study of Experimental Medicine* will be the revelation he is waiting for.

He was already acquainted with Darwin's theories of evolution, Dr. Lucas' *Treatise on Natural Heredity*, Taine's *Philosophy of Art;* but Claude Bernard's work will give him his permanent orientation. Zola's aim will be to introduce in the novel a scientific severity equal to that of the scientists. The literature of the second half of the nineteenth century will be characterized by the experimental novel, and its Claude Bernard will be Émile Zola.

Naïvely, he assumes that anarchy must be done away with. Up till now writers have written haphazardly, following what they called inspiration and giving little or no thought to the quality of the books they wrote. Such disorganization must cease. Novelists must never again be mere entertainers. No doubt a few have escaped this pitfall, but quite by chance. Balzac, Duranty, Flaubert, the Goncourt brothers, and, in a way, Stendhal are pretty much in the clear. But they are exceptional cases. We ought not to trust them. As long as a method is lacking, the worst can happen; incoherence threatens literature. Past disorder must end; the scientist in his laboratory, the novelist at his desk, will pursue the same goal: to know reality. What Claude Bernard has done for the body, Émile Zola will do for the passions, for the social classes; he will show that man is not an autonomous being, an individual mystery, the product of accidents, but the end result of a set of phenomena which, once they have been carefully studied, are sufficient to explain man and paint an exact picture of him. Here begins the vogue of the experimental novel.

Zola is thirty years old when he conceives the project of his *Natural and Social History of a Second Empire Family* (*Histoire naturelle et sociale d'une famille sous le Seconde Empire*). It is 1870, and the scientific rage has seized the whole world, or almost. No miracle is impossible for the sciences; the human condition is about to experience an unprecedented prosperity; progress is here to stay, the sky is the limit. Through a microscope, the eyes of the world peer into the future. Everything falls into order, once and for all; experimental medicine, the theory of the milieu, evolution, heredity, historical materialism, all have caught man in so tight a net that it is difficult to imagine how he can escape.

Zola's natural self-assurance is bolstered by such an extraordinary era. Undoubtedly, never before has anyone been so strongly convinced that he came by at the right moment, been so certain of being a child of his age. Zola is convinced of it to an incredible degree, and he shares unreservedly the faith his age has in the power of science to solve any problem. This

Les Rougon-Macquart

Histoire naturelle et sociale d'une famille sous le second Empire

I

LA FORTUNE DES ROUGON

PAR

ÉMILE ZOLA

PARIS
LIBRAIRIE INTERNATIONALE
A. LACROIX, VERBOECKHOVEN ET Cie, ÉDITEURS
15, boulevard Montmartre et faubourg Montmartre, 13
MÊME MAISON A BRUXELLES, A LEIPZIG ET A LIVOURNE

MDCCCLXXI
Tous droits de traduction et de reproduction réservés

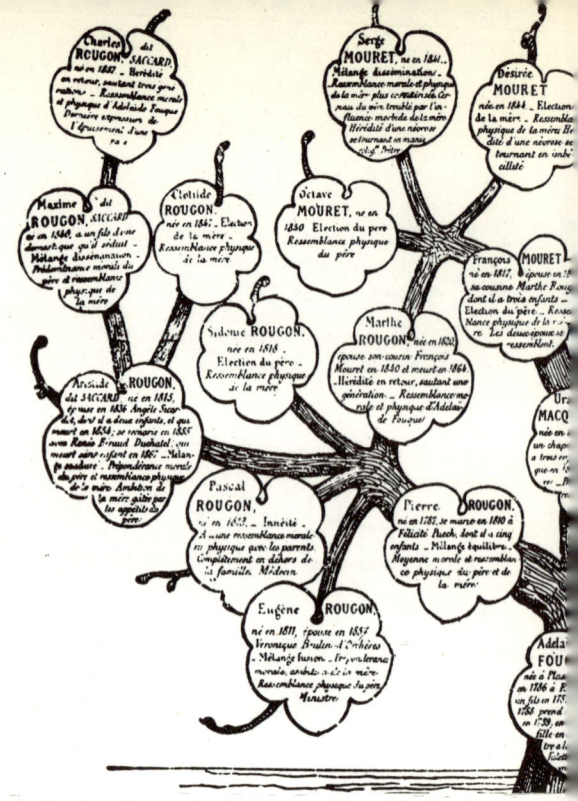

leads him to conclude that the task of the novelist will simply be to show the defects of society in order to enable the politicians to determine and apply the suitable remedies.

Claude Bernard, however, had denounced in advance such a generalized interpretation of his theories, as if he had foreseen the unintelligent use that might be made of them; he had established precisely the difference which seemed to him to oppose scientific works to those of the imagination, the objective world to the primarily subjective universe of literature.

Let us not smile too quickly. Did we not witness twenty-five years ago a similar enthusiasm among writers when they discovered psychoanalysis? Zola's ingenuousness was of the same nature, with the slight difference that his systematic mind attempted to carry the theory through to the very end. It is miraculous that certain ideas which seem to us today so rudimentary and even in many ways ludicrous enabled Zola to write masterpieces. Once more a mirage will have been more fertile than reality.

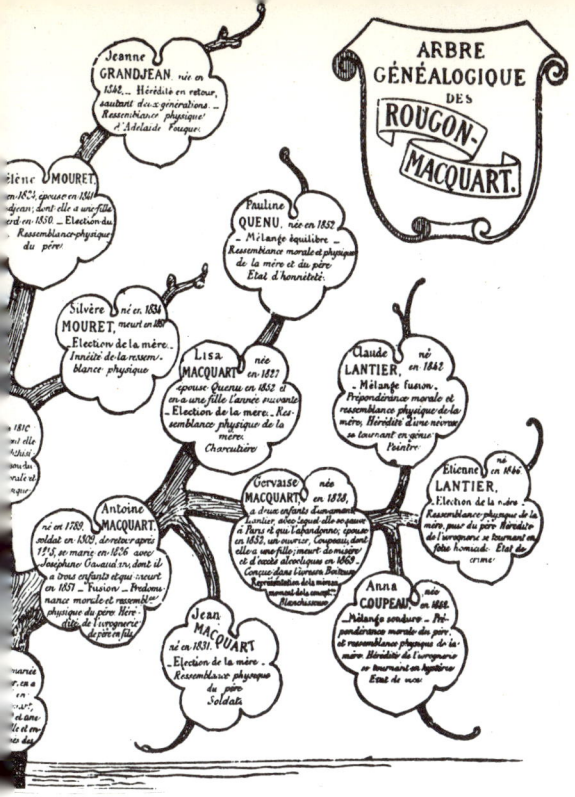

Engrossed in his discovery, Zola foresees at a single glance the series of novels which will make him famous. For a whole year, he goes to libraries; there he acquires, as he says, "a strong smattering of philosophy." And he works at the genealogical tree of the *Rougon-Macquart,* of which each branch will be a book. He feels his masterwork within his grasp.

But it is not enough to dream about it, he must write it; and this long-range task demands peace of mind. To whom will he turn? Lacroix is bankrupt; Zola goes to Charpentier and presents his project. The editor asks for two days to think it over and then accepts. The young writer's self-confidence has

39

once more been proved justified, nothing can stop him. Charpentier's contract is a considerable one: he will pay his new author five hundred francs a month for a great number of years. Yet Zola has not been able to reach the public at large, and there is nothing to assure him that his audience will grow appreciably. Charpentier was shrewd, however, and he must have liked to take chances.

With his material well-being comfortably assured, Zola had nothing to do but set to work; we can imagine the burst of energy with which this man who wanted "to eat mountains" throws himself into his task. For the first time he has no other worry except to create; he feels it necessary to set himself a schedule in order to carry out his project: he will rise at eight, take an hour-long walk if the weather permits; then from nine until one in the afternoon he will write the same number of pages every day.

Working for a certain number of regular hours, whatever the mood, cannot help but lead to an enormous amount of waste; it means rejecting any kind of critical appraisal; it involves assuming that the daily production is consistently good. It is a completely Western concept of a work of art, wholly opposed to that of the fifteenth-century Chinese painter who had written in a corner of his *kakemono*: "It took me ten years to paint this landscape, but I devoted to it only my moments of happiness."

Flatness, then, does not frighten Zola; with an even motion he carries forward the best and the worst, and the work of the morning is added to the work of the day before, the good propping up the mediocre, as if each page were only a set distance to overcome.

The only disturbance to his work will be due to the war. Literature is for a time of little consequence. Zola seeks shelter in Bordeaux, where he was almost made prefect of the *département*. The Government for National Defense had made him vice-prefect of Castelsarrasin, but Gambetta did not sanction the nomination. On September 29, 1870, Zola writes to Valabrègue: "They promise me a position as prefect in the next prefectoral change. I shall decide then what I should do."

As a matter of fact he has something better to do, and he does not wait long before going back to Paris. Of course, his scientific serenity is not perfect. For each of his novels the hours of anguish will outnumber the hours of joy. Zola finds reassurance and solace only after he has written the last line. Then he breathes, stretches, sends a victory bulletin to his friends, his editor. It is an ephemeral truce, however, for the new novel is already there with its new demands. From one to the other, he has barely time to catch his breath, to set out again in search of materials; then the work begins again, either in Paris, in Médan, or at the seashore. And in order to better remember his promise, Émile Zola orders inscribed in gold letters on the mantelpiece opposite his desk at Médan: *Nulla dies sine linea.* Never was a promise better kept.

In a speech addressed to students a little while before his death, Zola will say that his only reason for living has been work, that it was in work that he found all his joy. He writes as a river rises and gradually drowns all the obstacles it meets. He has neither Hugo's genius nor the purity of his language. Each page of *Les Misérables* is brightened by a poetry which magnifies everything; thus illuminated each detail begins to resemble a jewel. Émile Zola is humble in nature, his equipment is unrefined, misuse of language abounds in his books; but in his way he will save himself, his power will compensate for all his deficiencies, the magnitude of his vision will help him live down his imperfections. He has the cardinal virtue of strength.

Two giants preceded him; the shadows of Hugo and Balzac hover over the literature of nineteenth-century France. *The Human Comedy* has shown all aspects of a society which cannot have changed too much during the following thirty years. The likes of Rastignac, Rubempré, Vautrin, Père Goriot still move about in the salons, the shops, the lower levels of society. Balzac had taken a complete census, explored every region; he seems to have left to his successors nothing but the possibility of mere repetition. To be sure, Zola would need only to see the world from a different angle in order to produce an original contribution, but his approach is very similar to Balzac's. The author of *Thérèse Raquin* is also an investigator, he too is burning with the desire to make a complete inventory of society. More so even, it is for him a necessity, for he is deprived of a certain depth – such as that in which Dostoevsky moves about with such ease. On the other hand, he could never vie with the author of *The Human Comedy* in the knowledge of passions. He tries nonetheless, but with the anguish of having before him a much too perfect example.

Les Misérables, on the other hand, was published ten years before the first volume of the *Rougon-Macquart*. And that book rises like an enormous edifice with its double barricade, its crowds of rioters, Valjean's epic wandering through a network of sewers, its thousand scenes in the streets of Paris, its characters, rough-hewn by an amazingly powerful hand, who, by a transmutation of genius, gain in symbolic value what they lose in nuance.

With these two writers always present in his thoughts, Émile Zola must clear a way for himself. As he begins the series of the *Rougon-Macquart,* Zola explicitly assigns himself several objectives: to be original, to revolutionize literature, to raise himself to the level of his illustrious predecessors. Salvation will come with completion; the finished work rises and shines in the distance, a work which could not spring up out of a moment of sudden inspiration, in the fever of some propitious days, but a work which must be built hour after hour. Zola is thirty when he begins, and it is understandable that he has no time to lose.

The first two volumes appear in 1871: *The Rougons' Luck, (La Fortune des Rougon)* and *The Quarry (La Curée).* As soon as the second is published the battle begins. The Attorney General of the Republic receives a large number of letters of denunciation.

Since the novel appears as a serial in *La Cloche,* Zola suggests to the editor that he discontinue publication in the newspaper. But he defends himself in these words:

> *The Quarry* is not an isolated book, it is part of a large work, it is but a musical phrase in the vast symphony of which I dream. I want to write *The Natural and Social History of a Family during the Second Empire.* The first episode, called *The Rougons' Luck,* has just been published; it tells of Napoleon III's *coup d'état* and the brutal rape of France. The other episodes will depict the morals and manners of every part of society, they will deal with the politics of the period, its finances, its courts of justice, its military life, its churches, its institutionalized public depravity. I wish to point out, on the other hand, that the first episode was published by *Le Siècle* during the imperial regime, and that I had no idea that an attorney general of the Republic would some day hinder me in my work. For three years I assembled information; filth, incredible ad-

ventures of shame and folly, stolen money and women for sale, those were the overpowering facts, ever-present before my eyes. That note of gold and of flesh, the note of trickling millions and of the increasing noise of orgies was sounded so loudly and so continuously that I decided to sing it. I wrote *The Quarry*. Should I have kept quiet; could I have left in the dark that glitter of debauchery which shows the Second Empire in an evil light? Were I to do so, I should obscure the story I wish to write.

Louis Ulbach, the editor, nevertheless joined his readers; he declares Zola obscene. How many times will Zola hear that accusation! Later on he will shrug his shoulders, but for now he is indignant. On September 9, 1872 he writes:

> Ah! my dear Ulbach, it is all I can do to keep from answering with an artist's anger the letter you wrote to Guérin who showed it to me! "Obscene!" So it is that word again! I get it from your pen as I have heard it from M. Prudhomme's mouth. You were incapable of finding another word to judge me, and it makes me think that that foul word did not come from you, that you have let somebody slip it into your pocket in some governmental office in order to stick it piping hot under my nose.
> Oh! That word! If you only knew how stupid I think it is. Forgive me, but I am speaking to you as a colleague and not as one of your writers. Fortunately, it does not enrage me any more, since I have heard it from the imperial attorney generals. No, you have not hurt me, although "obscene" is terribly foul. I am going to burn your letter to keep this quarrel from posterity. I know that you will take back the word "obscene" when the ladies quit setting you against me.

The accusation of obscenity haunts Zola. A few years later, in his essay entitled *Of Morality in Literature,* he defends himself in this manner:

> For me, the question of talent determines everything in literature. I don't understand what is meant by a moral or an immoral writer; but I know very well the difference between a writer who has talent and one who hasn't any. And, as soon as an author has talent, I feel that anything is

allowed him. History speaks for itself. We gave Rabelais complete freedom in France just as they gave Shakespeare freedom in England. A well-written page has its own morality in its beauty, in the intensity of its life and of its tone. It is stupid to want to subject it to fashionable conventions, to a craze for virtue. I believe that the only obscene works are the ill-inspired and ill-performed ones.

And a little further:

As I have already mentioned, our works are too gloomy, too cruel to hit the public in the right way and please it. They repel rather than captivate. While it is true that a few of them sell well, the majority leave book buyers upset and indignant. Beginners who deliberately try to paint human infamy will soon meet with terrible disappointments. First of all, they will realize that sincerity is indispensable; one must love truth – and have a lot of talent – in order to dare paint it plain and naked without falling into the vile and the odious. Then they will realize that real hypocrisy leads more directly to fame and fortune than does an affectation of brutality. Hypocrisy is pampered and handsomely rewarded; while brutality makes enemies of most people, who are embarrassed by frankness. If that brutality, that audacity to leave nothing unsaid are not part of the writer's temperament, it quickly becomes obvious that the writer is calculating, and he will be almost immediately scorned, and rightfully so. In short, I mean that calculated dishonesty presents no danger, for the crowd is always ready to approve and be moved; while calculated truthfulness, on the contrary, is a death trap where a mercenary author always ends up by breaking his neck. That is why, if they are not guided by their temperament, the clever ones do well to work with virtue rather than vice.

From 1871 to 1876, Émile Zola publishes six volumes: *The Rougons' Luck, The Quarry, The Bowels of Paris (Le Ventre de Paris), The Conquest of Plassans (La Conquête de Plassans),* Abbé Mouret's Transgression *(La Faute de l'Abbé Mouret),* His Excellency Eugène Rougon (Son Excellence Eugène Rougon). He is now thirty-six years old. His capacity for work is astonishing, as is the breadth of his ambition; the critics receive his novels with interest; the books are discussed, even though the author's theories provoke some smiles, but success is still not assured. Victor Hugo may scorn the attacks of the leader of the naturalistic school, because he continues to dominate his era; no one has yet doubted his supremacy.

Toward his friends, Zola remains faithful to the team spirit which he professed in his youth. Among his contemporaries he has chosen his master: Flaubert; he has made friends of Edmond de Goncourt and Alphonse Daudet. The group sometimes lunches out together. Zola eats well, for he is fond of food, but he speaks little and badly, except when he gets excited about a subject close to his heart, or when he is answering questions about the book on which he is working. His friends do not take his theory of the experimental novel seriously, nor the laws of heredity applied to the novel; they laugh up their sleeves and let his disarming candor amuse them. But they treat with respect the power inherent in this companion who fills the newspapers as far as distant Russia with his articles, and whose courage and capacity for controversy no one questions.

There is a phrase that they like to hear him say, and that the mischievous Daudet loves to make him repeat: "I am chaste." His little speech defect adds an amusing touch to it. The fact that they tease him does not keep his friends from thinking highly of Zola whose work is beginning to surprise them by its scope.

The author of *The Rougon-Macquart* takes advantage of those meals to obtain information about some of the social circles he does not know well. He has never been in high society; the upper bourgeoisie, the aristocracy are foreign to him; he tries to supplement his knowledge through the confidences of Flaubert who has mingled at the imperial court, as well as through those of de Goncourt and Daudet. He remembers no doubt that Balzac used exactly the same means.

Furthermore, these authors feel a deep solidarity among themselves; they all belong, whether they like it or not, and in various degrees, to the naturalistic school. The painter Courbet started the expression "naturalism," and the public uses it to designate writers of such varied temperaments as Flaubert, Goncourt, Daudet, and Zola; together they form a group which is hated, feared, envied. Each of them is conscious of the advantages to be gained from such solidarity. Here again Zola's powerful personality, his passion for struggle and controversy, helped considerably in the formation of the group.

Caricature by André Gill in *La Lune rousse* (The Red Moon)

The Dram-shop (l'Assommoir)

As early as August 14, 1875, Zola informs Charpentier, his editor, of his project for a new novel for which he has no set title, and which will be *The Dram-shop*. Daydreaming at a window overlooking the ocean at Saint-Aubin, Zola foresees the importance of this work which will make him famous.

My dear friend, I must absolutely let you hear from me. I am not guilty of laziness, I assure you. I am working a lot; I surprise myself with the wise and steady way I stay at the improvised desk I have set up by a window. I must admit that I have the open sea in front of me. The boats do disturb me a little. I sit long minutes at a time following the sails, with my pen fallen out of my hand. But every day I write my Marseille correspondence; I am writing a large study on the Goncourts for Russia, I am even planning my next novel, that novel about the people, which I dream will be extraordinary.

The Dram-shop appears as a serial during the autumn of 1876, and already Zola hears from Albert Millaud the very criticisms which will recur over and over again about this book. They elicit from him this reply:

Gervaise attendant Lantier
1

La Bataille de Gervaise et de Virginie
2

Coupeau et Gervaise à l'assommoir
3

Repas de noce d Coupeau et de Gervaise

L'accident de Coupeau

Duel de Gouget et de [illegible]

L'ASSOMMOIR

La fête de Gervaise
7

Gervaise et Lantier trouvant Coupeau ivre-mort
8

Gervaise venant chercher Coupeau à l'assommoir
9

Gervaise chez Goujet
10

Delirium tremens de Coupeau
11

Mort de Gervaise
12

You call me a democratic and somewhat socialistic writer, and you wonder at my depicting the working class in its true gloomy colors.

First of all, I do not accept the label you paste on my back. I mean to be a novelist, purely and simply, without any qualifying adjective; if you insist upon qualifying me, say that I am a naturalistic novelist, which will not annoy me. My political views are not in question, and the journalist who may be in me has no bone to pick with the novelist who is me. People should read my novels, read them without prejudice, understand them and see the total picture they present before they pass the odious and grotesque ready-made judgments that are going around about me and my works. Ah, if you knew how much fun my friends make of the astounding legend handed out to the crowd every time my name appears in a newspaper! If you knew the extent to which the blood-thirsty, ferocious novelist is an honest bourgeois, a learned artist, living quietly in his corner with his own convictions! I don't deny any tale, I work, I leave to time and the good faith of the public the task of finally uncovering me from under the heap of foolishness.

As for my portrayal of the working class, it is such as I wanted it, without a shadow, without toning down. I tell what I see, all I do is put it into words, and I let the moralists draw the lessons. I have laid bare the wounds of high society, I am certainly not going to hide those of the lower classes. My work is not the work of a party nor of propaganda; it is a work of truth.

The year of its publication in book form, 1877, is also the year which will assure his success. The repercussions of the book are such that Zola becomes the most famous of French writers; a few weeks are enough to make his name popular. For the first time in almost a half century, Hugo drops into second place; a thirty-seven-year-old writer gets the better of the old poet. The stir created earlier by *Les Misérables* is outdone.

Because he was the first to make workers the characters of a novel, Zola caught his readers unawares. The proletariat, increased every day by the progress of the machine age, was still without a face or a voice; industrial cities were springing up from the ground, craftsmen were losing their identity in the anonymous army of the mills and the factories. But the writers were looking elsewhere: the boudoir, financial discussions, social ambitions, crimes of passion were just about the only things to hold their attention.

Zola is the first to look at what is coming. He is of his time, sometimes naively and excessively so, but he emerges out of it better than anyone else: he sees further ahead. He is completely taken by that gloomy world, echoing the new roar of modern times, that apocalyptic aspect of the industrialization of the world. In two volumes he denounces one of the vices of the working classes at that time: alcoholism. And for the first time, he conveys an idea of his full force. The color and the depth of the work are admirable; the spell is complete; the blacks achieve the intensity of an engraving, the center bright with a single diabolical light, the fires of alcohol.

Gervaise's downfall, the neighborhood where she lives, the Paris landscapes seen from the heights of Montmartre and the swarming drinkers around the bars, the listlessness which eventually numbs all of them except the blacksmith – that picture of hell is grandiose.

The Dram-shop is the prototype, the unequaled masterpiece of the *roman noir*. The skies are cloudy, the streets are pictured mostly at night; there is never or almost never any sun; no rays of light, not even those that pierce the shadows in Rembrandt's etchings; everything is black as tar, poignantly ugly. The characters lose their human traits; numbness deprives them of all human attributes, they are heading for the gutter. With relentless cruelty, Zola keeps after his heroine, Gervaise, and releases her only when she is dead, after he has shown her to us in her mud-spattered dress, in slippers, vainly trying to prostitute herself.

And yet, out of those countless horrors rises a strange beauty; the power of such a picture has a certain hypnotic force. The wonder is that a man has had the courage to write such a book, to fulfill his intention completely without a moment of weakening, and that he has found colors strong enough to paint such a picture.

Zola's great interest in painting is known, as is his ability to judge it, with the sole exception of that of Cézanne, his childhood friend, whose work, paradoxically, he did not understand. Actually, such a lack of understanding seems peculiar only on the surface, for no two men were ever more different than they. To Cézanne reality is the reflection of a more complex truth of which we grasp only the image, and while the painter insists on interpreting it as faithfully as possible, his soul is elsewhere. He believes in a transcendental truth, while for his friend Zola there is no other truth than the one he can observe. While both of them agree that they must express "reality," the meaning which each gives to it is radically opposed to the other. It is no wonder then that their differences were to lead to the breakup of their friendship. It is the same kind of misunderstanding which will divide Huysmans and Zola.

But aside from this error, the majority of the other painters whom Zola was one of the first to defend – and with what passion! – are the ones whom we recognize today as some of the greatest of their day.

This taste for painting is noticeable in each page of *The Dram-shop*. Zola writes as if he were painting; as one says, a painter *manqué*.

We know only too well that writers have often used satire and eroticism supposedly to castigate our morals; today they do not claim to speak in the name of morality but in the name of truth which some of them call, in the words of Zola, "the savage part of man," while others call it "the whole man." Today we are still fully in the age of the experimental novel; except for a few exceptions we remain within the naturalistic school. Never has a novelist had more descendants; anything worthwhile in the novel owes something to Zola.

Improving upon Balzac, he has, with *The Dram-shop*, taken literature to the depths of gloom; it is in vain that his successors will endeavor to do better: he reaches the limits of darkness. Since the *Inferno* and a few Shakespearian tragedies, nobody had dared probe so deeply into the horror that the human condition can inspire.

The unhappiness of his characters is due more to their complete lack of energy than to the conditions imposed upon them; each of them carries in the most secret part of himself a frightfully strong seed of self-destruction. The evil is in the human being; circumstances are very unimportant; a man needs only to fail to resist, and he finds himself dragged to the lowest depths. Zola has been able to render such scenes as the Monday morning chats at the bar, the tool box sliding down from a shoulder to the floor, the feeling of slipping into the irrevocable, the fascination with destruction, with an admirably accurate tone.

Were there but a ray of light in the corner of the picture, we would have a Christian book; but grace is banned from Zola's work more drastically even than from Balzac's. Man is alone, helpless, hopeless, sinless, wandering in the dark, not even calling out, reduced to mere animality, traveling through life never taking his eyes off the ground, like an animal going to die. When he is accused of giving such a hopeless picture of man, Zola, who is incapable of any metaphysical reflection, can only justify such a vision of hell by his repeated condemnation of the slums.

We cannot say that his understanding is short-sighted, since he can show us with such realism the feelings and temperaments of those unfortunate people. The hand wins over the head, talent over careful consideration. Zola's naive ambition of building a scientific work keeps him from seeing beyond that point; he loses the most valuable part and keeps only the elements of that total man whom he claims to present. Social classes, environment are sufficient answers to him. Zola's novels are also full of madmen, but heredity and sociology seem to him to be adequate explanations of their condition. It is as if his psychological gifts exhaust themselves as soon as he leaves his characters in order to judge his work.

The workers were the most indignant when *The Dram-shop* was published, while the bourgeoisie were overjoyed. The former refused to recognize themselves in a portrayal that seemed to them both base and false; the latter grabbed the opportunity to despise those whom they were beginning to fear.

The reason is that Zola is in no way a demagogue, he does not tone down defects, he underlines them rather, not worried about what the model will think of it.

Here is the scene in which Coupeau, influenced by Lantier, is beginning to miss work. From now on his downfall will gather speed.

> Coupeau hesitated for an instant; and then, quietly, as though he had only made up his mind after considerable reflection, he set his bag on the floor, saying: "It's too late now. I'll go to Bourguignon's after lunch. I'll tell him that the missus was ill. Listen, old Colombe, I'll leave my tools under this seat, and I'll call for them at twelve o'clock."
>
> Lantier nodded his approval of this arrangement. A man must work, no doubt; only, when he is with friends, politeness

passes before everything. An inclination for a spree had gradually overcome the four of them, and they stood there with heavy hands, and exchanging questioning glances. And as soon as they realized that they had five hours' idleness before them, they were suddenly seized with a noisy joy, catching each other friendly slaps, and bawling affectionate words in each other's faces. Coupeau, who in particular felt much relieved and even younger, called the others "old bricks!" They had one more round of drinks, and then moved off to the "Sniffing Flea," a low dram-shop which possessed a billiard table. The hatter at first made a grimace, for it was not a very clean-looking crib; the brandy there cost a franc the quart, ten sous a pint in two glasses, and the customers had so soiled the billiard table that the balls fairly stuck to it. However, when once the game had begun, the hatter, who was an extremely expert player, recovered his good temper and graciousness, thrusting his chest forward and wriggling his hips at each cannon he made.

When lunch time came, Coupeau had an idea. He stamped his feet and exclaimed: "We must go to fetch Salted-Chops. I know where he works. We'll take him to Mother Louis's to have some stewed pettitoes."

The idea was greeted with acclamations. Yes, Salted-Chops, otherwise Drink-without-Thirst, must be in want of some pettitoes. So they started off. The streets were yellowish, and a fine rain was falling. But the tipplers were already too warm internally to feel a slight watering of their limbs. Coupeau led the others to the bolt factory in the Rue Marcadet, and as they arrived there a good half hour before the time when the workmen usually came out, he gave a lad a couple of sous to go in and tell Salted-Chops that his wife was ill and wanted him at once. The blacksmith made his appearance, strutting along but looking very calm, and already scenting a tuck-out.

"Ah! you jokers!" said he, as soon as he caught sight of the others hiding in a doorway. "I guessed as much. Well! what are we going to eat?"

Once at Mother Louis's, whilst they sucked the little bones of the pettitoes, they again fell to abusing the employer class. Salted-Chops, otherwise Drink-without-Thirst, related that at his crib they just then had a most pressing order to execute. So the boss was fairly pleasant for the time being. One might be late, and he dared say nothing; he no doubt considered himself lucky when the men did turn up. Besides, there was no fear that any one would ever dare to give Salted-Chops the sack, for it was no longer possible to find fellows of his talent in the bolt-forging line. Then, the pettitoes having been disposed of, the company ordered an omelet. Each drank his quart of wine. Mother Louis had her wine sent to her from Auvergne – it was of blood-like hue, and could almost be cut with a knife. Things were now beginning to get amusing; the carouse was going apace.

"What do you think is the boss's latest?" cried Salted-Mouth at dessert. "Why, he's been and put a bell up in his crib! A bell, indeed! that's good for slaves. Ah well! it can ring today! They won't catch me at the anvil again! I've been sticking there for five days past, and may well give myself a rest. If he has the cheek to fine me, I'll send him to blazes."

"For my part," said Coupeau, with an important air, "I'm obliged to leave you; I'm off to work. Yes, I promised my wife – Amuse yourselves; my heart, you know, remains with my pals."

The others chaffed him. But he seemed so decided that at last they all accompanied him on his way to fetch his tools from old Colombe's. He there took his bag from under the seat and laid it on the floor before him, whilst they had a final drink. But at one o'clock the party was still standing glasses round. Then Coupeau, with a gesture of boredom, once more deposited the tools under the seat. They were in his way; he could not get near the counter without stumbling against them. It was all too absurd to think of working that day; he would go to Bourguignon's on the morrow.

One evening on payday, Gervaise has gone to wait for her husband at the door of "l'Assommoir." Seeing that he was not coming out, she went in to join him, and for the first time she begins to drink.

"Ah, well!" cried Coupeau, suddenly turning his wife's empty glass upside down, "you get rid of it pretty quickly. Just look, you others, she doesn't take long over it, does she?"

"Will madame take another?" asked Salted-Chops, otherwise Drink-without-Thirst.

No, she had had enough. Yet she hesitated. The aniseed seemed to have a sickening effect. She would rather have taken something stiffer to keep her hungry stomach quiet. And she glanced askance at the fuddling machine near her. The sight of that horrible pot-bellied cauldron, with its long twisted nose, sent a shiver down her back, a commingling of fear and desire. You might have thought the thing to be some round fat witch slowly throwing off liquid fire. A fine poison source it was, a brazen abomination which ought to have been hidden away in a cellar! But all the same Gervaise would have liked to poke her nose inside it, sniff and taste its contents, even if in doing so the skin should peel off her burnt tongue like the rind off an orange.

"What's that you're drinking?" she slyly asked the men, her eyes brightening as she noticed the beautiful golden colour of the liquid in their glasses.

"That, old woman," answered Coupeau, "is papa Colombe's camphor. Now don't be stupid, we'll just let you taste it."

And when they had brought her a glass of the "vitriol," and her jaws contracted at the first mouthful, the zinc-worker resumed, slapping his thighs: "Eh! it tickles your gullet! Come, drink it off at a go. Each glassful cheats the doctor of six francs."

At the second glass, Gervaise no longer felt the hunger which had been tormenting her. She was now good friends again with Coupeau, no longer angry with him for having failed to keep his word. They would also go to the circus some other day; after all it was not so funny to see a lot of mountebanks galloping about on horses. There was no rain inside old Colombe's, and if the money did go in brandy, one at least had it in one's body; one drank it limpid, glittering like beautiful liquid gold. Ah! she was ready to send the whole world to blazes! Life didn't offer so many pleasures; besides, it seemed to her some consolation to have her share in squandering the cash. As she was comfortable, why shouldn't she remain? There might be a discharge of artillery; for her part she never cared to stir, once she had settled down. She was simmering as it were in what seemed to her a pleasant warmth, her bodice clinging to her back, whilst a sensation of comfort stole through her, benumbing her limbs. She laughed all to herself, her elbows resting on the table, and a vacant look in her eyes, as she gazed, highly amused, at two customers, a fat heavy fellow and a dwarf, who sat at a neighbouring table, so very drunk that they were actually kissing one another. Yes, she laughed at the "Assommoir," at old Colombe's full moon face, at the customers smoking, yelling and spitting, and at the big gas flames which set the looking-glasses and bottles of liqueurs fairly ablaze. The smell no longer inconvenienced her; on the contrary, it tickled her nose, and she thought it very pleasant. Her eyes closed somewhat whilst she breathed very slowly, but without the least feeling of oppression, enjoying indeed the gentle slumber which was overcoming her. Then, after her third glass, she let her chin fall on her hands, and saw nothing apart from Coupeau and his mates, with whom she remained cheek by jowl, warmed by their breath, and gazing at their dirty beards as though she were counting the hairs. They were very drunk by this time. My-Boots, his pipe still between his teeth, was drivelling with the dumb grave air of a dozing ox. Bibi-the-Smoker was telling how he emptied a quart bottle at a draught, while Salted-Chops, otherwise Drink-without-Thirst, went to fetch the wheel of fortune from the counter, in order to play Coupeau for drinks.

And here is Gervaise at the lowest degree of her downfall. Half dead from hunger, abandoned by her husband, she is going to try to prostitute herself.

Gervaise stood in front of the "Assommoir," thinking that if she had only possessed a couple of sous she could have gone inside for a nip. A nip no doubt would have quieted her hunger. Ah! what a number of nips she had drunk in her time! Liquor seemed good stuff to her after all. And from outside she watched the fuddling machine, realising that her misfortunes came from it, and yet dreaming of finishing herself off with brandy whenever she should have some cash. But a shudder passed through her hair, as she saw that it was now quite dark. She must show some courage if she didn't wish to croak amidst the general revelry. The sight of other people gorging didn't precisely fill her own maw. She slackened her pace again, and looked around her. There was a darker shade under the trees. Only few people passed, folks in a hurry who swiftly crossed the Boulevards. But on the broad, dark, deserted, central footwalk, where the sound of the revelry died away, women stood for long moments motionless, as stiff-looking as the scrubby little plane trees beside them. Then they slowly began to move, dragging their slippers over the frozen soil, taking ten steps or so and then halting once more. There was one with a huge frame and insect-like limbs who swayed about in a black silk rag, with a yellow scarf over her head; there was another tall and bony, bareheaded and wearing a servant's apron; and others, too – both old and young. And Gervaise tried to imitate them, though an attack of girlish emotion contracted her throat. She seemed to be living in a horrible dream. For a quarter of an hour she remained standing erect, but people hurried by without even turning their heads. Then she in her turn moved about, and as a man passed near her whistling, with his hands in his pockets, she murmured in a strangled voice: "Sir, just listen."

The man gave her a side glance and then went off, whistling all the louder.

Then Gervaise grew bolder, the hunger which gripped and tortured her, urging her into this wild chase for a meal, the chance of which seemed to grow fainter and fainter. For a long while she walked about, without thinking of the flight of time or of the direction she took. Around her the dark mute women went to and fro under the trees like wild beasts in a cage. Whenever they passed a gas-lamp they emerged from the shade like apparitions; then as they went off into the darkness they grew vague once more. Now and again some individual halted, jested with them, and then walked away, laughing. There was a deal of murmuring, of quarrelling in undertones, which suddenly gave place to silence. And as far as Gervaise went she saw these women standing at intervals like sentinels; they seemed to be posted along the whole length of the Boulevards. All Paris was encompassed by them. For her part, in her sore need of bread, she again and again ragefully changed her place, finally walking up and down between the Chaussée Clignancourt and the Grande Rue of La Chapelle.

"Sir, just listen."

But those whom she addressed passed by. She started from the slaughterhouses, which reeked of blood; she glanced on her way at the old Hotel Boncoeur, now closed; she passed in front of the Lariboisière Hospital, and mechanically counted the windows which were illumined by a pale quiet glimmer, like that of night-lights at the bedsides of agonising sufferers. And she also crossed the railway bridge, beneath which the trains rushed with a noisy rumble, rending the air atwain with their shrill whistling. Ah! how sad did everything seem at night-time! Then she turned on her heels again, and filled her eyes with the sight of the same houses, doing this ten and twenty times without pausing, without resting for a minute on a bench. But none would listen to her. Her shame seemed to be increased by this contempt. Nevertheless, she went down towards the hospital again, and then returned towards the slaughterhouses. It was her last promenade – from the blood-stained yards, where animals were stricken low, to the pale hospital wards, where death was stiffening the patients stretched between the sheets. It was between these limits that she had passed her life.

"Sir, just listen."

But suddenly she perceived her shadow on the ground. Whenever she came near to a gas-lamp it gradually drew itself together, became less vague, more clearly defined, and terrible grotesque, so portly had she nowadays grown. And such, moreover, was her lameness that the shadow seemed to turn a somersault at every step she took. It looked like a real Punch! Then as she left the lamp behind her, the Punch grew taller, becoming in fact gigantic, filling the whole Boulevard, and bobbing to and fro in such a style that it seemed likely to smash its nose against the trees or the houses. Good heavens! how frightful she was! Never before had she realised her disfigurement so thoroughly. And from that moment she could not refrain from looking at her shadow; she even waited for the gas-lamps, ever watching the bobbing of that Punch-like reflection. Ah! she had a pretty companion with her! What a figure! It could scarcely be attractive! And at the thought of her unsightliness, she lowered her voice, and scarcely dared to stammer: "Sir, Just listen."

Among the writers of Zola's time, it is not surprising that J. K. Huysmans expressed the most favorable judgment:

> Ah! you may scream, roar, blush if you can, say that *The Dram-shop* is for the rabble and the riff-raff, say that coarse words stagger you, what of it! the artists, the literate are in seventh heaven. . . .

7ᵐᵉ ANNÉE — N° 325   PARIS ET DÉPARTEMENTS : 15 CENTIMES LE NUMÉRO   1ᵉʳ JUILLET 1877

LE GRELOT

L'ASSOMMOIR & LA FILLE ÉLISA PAR PÉPIN

Ou l'Art de se faire 3,000 livres de rente en démoralisant ses concitoyens.

... and finally these extraordinary pages which, later when Zola's glory will remain unquestioned, will be counted among the most beautiful, the most dazzling of our literature: Lalie's death and Gervaise's walking the streets. Is it possible that some people dare deny this man's priceless talent, his powerful personality, his breadth, his strength, unique in this age of weakness and languor.... (*L'Actualité de Bruxelles, 1876.*)

But perhaps the following lines written by Mallarmé to Zola are more noteworthy:

Here is indeed a great work; and worthy of a period when truth becomes the popular form of beauty! Those who accuse you of not having written for the people are mistaken in a way, as much as those who regret a former ideal; you have found a modern one, that is all. The gloomy ending of the book and your attempt at linguistic reform, thanks to which so many expressions, often inept when they are coined by poor writers, take on the value of the most beautiful literary phrases since they are capable of making us literate men smile or nearly weep! That moves me indescribably; whether because of a natural disposition within me, however, or perhaps because of an even more difficult victory on your part, I know not. But the beginning of the novel remains so far the part which I prefer. The prodigiously sincere simplicity of the descriptions of the worker Coupeau or of the woman's shop keep me under a spell from which the sad events of the end cannot release me; you have endowed literature with something entirely new in those pages that turn quietly like the days of a lifetime. (A letter, February 3, 1877.)

For the first time, in any case, a talented writer was making contact with the working class, and from the repercussion of his work, novels were going to rise which would draw the attention of the world to the proletariat. In the face of *The Dram-shop's* success, Charpentier, showing integrity, modifies the terms of Zola's contract. The newspapers vie for the writer's future works; they offer from twenty to thirty thousand francs to publish them as serials. Thus it soon becomes possible for him to buy a house in Médan. He tells Flaubert about it in the following manner:

I have bought a house, a rabbit hutch, between Poissy and Triel, in a charming little hole along the banks of the Seine; nine thousand francs; I am telling you the price so that you will not be too impressed. Literature has paid for this modest shelter in the country, which has the merit of being far from any station and of counting not a single bourgeois in its neighborhood. I am alone, absolutely alone; for a month I have not seen a human face.

From now on money will not cease to pour in. Never has a house been more bound to a writer's reputation; both grew together. But instead of adding wings, Zola had towers built. Thus about 1880 the Nana tower was to rise, and about 1885 the Germinal tower. The success of Zola's works could be ascertained by looking in the direction of his house: the novels turned to stones.

The house was getting furnished also; blossoming with odds and ends or knickknacks bought haphazardly and with little taste in the antique shops. Impressed by Edmond de Goncourt's Japanese interior, Émile Zola attempted to compete with him in secondhand bargains; the result was not very happy. He had little time, on the other hand, to devote to such trifles; the *Rougon-Macquart's* genealogical tree was waiting for its gardener. There is nothing more unlimited than a family: all one has to do is to add descendants.

THE HOUSE IN MÉDAN
Photograph taken during Zola's lifetime

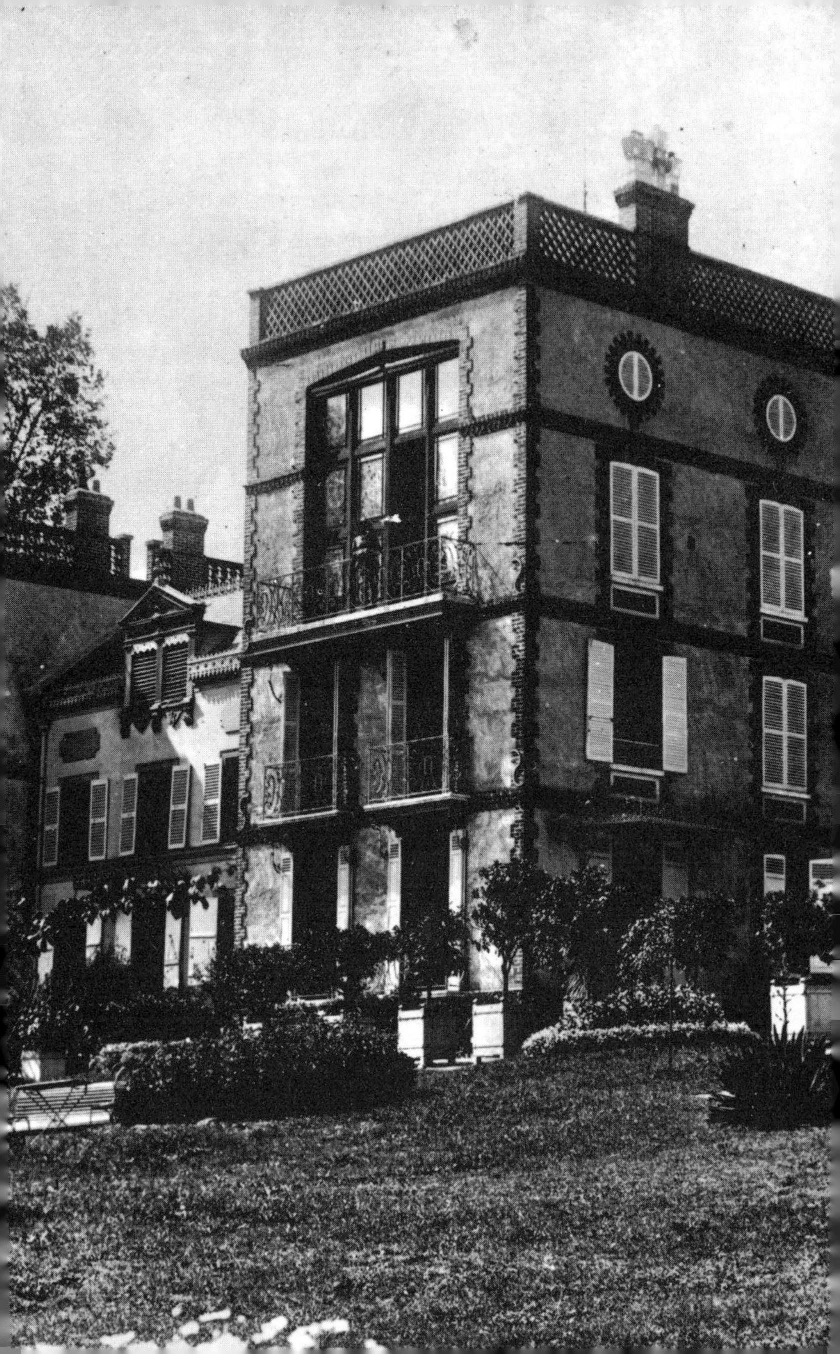

A caricature of 1878

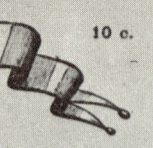

A Love Episode (Une page d'amour)

The Dram-shop had hardly been published when Zola set to work again, this time, however, to write a very different kind of book: *A Love Episode*. The contrast between this work and the preceding one amuses him. From L'Estaque, he writes to Théodore Duret in September, 1877: "What sustains me is the thought of the public's stupefaction in the face of such gentleness. I love to baffle my readers."

This is what he also tells J. K. Huysmans:

> I have just finished the first part of my novel, which is to have five parts. It is a little pedestrian, a little silly; but it will be swallowed pleasantly, I believe. I want to surprise the readers of *The Dram-shop,* with a simple, good-natured book. I am enchanted when I have written a good little page, naïve as a sixteen-year-old. Yet I do not say that, here and there, some stray vulgarity does not entice me into rather improper realms. But that is the exception. I am calling the readers to a family gathering where they will meet good-hearted souls. Well, the first part ends with a bird's-eye view of Paris, first drowned in the fog, then getting clearer and clearer under a golden spring sun, which is, I believe, one of best pages so far. That is why I am happy, and I say it, you see, in a lyrical tone.

Since Zola was so happy with those lines, here they are:

A haze was stealing over the outlying districts of Paris, whose immensity faded away in this pale, vague mist. Round the Trocadéro the city was of a leaden hue and lifeless, while the last snowflakes slowly fluttered down in pale specks against the gloomy background. Beyond the chimneys of the Army Bakehouse, the brick towers of which had a coppery tint, these white dots descended more thickly; a gauze seemed to be floating in the air, falling to earth thread by thread.

Not a breath stirred as the dream-like shower sleepily and rhythmically descended from the atmosphere. As they neared the roofs the flakes seemed to falter in their flight; in myriads they ceaselessly pillowed themselves on one another, in such intense silence that even blossoms shedding their petals make more noise; and from this moving mass, whose descent through space was inaudible, there sprang a sense of such intense peacefulness that earth and life were forgotten. A milky whiteness spread more and more over the whole heavens though they were still darkened here and there by wreaths of smoke. Little by little, bright clusters of houses became plainly visible; a bird's-eye view was obtained of the whole city, intersected by streets and squares, which with their shadowy depths described the framework of the several districts.

. . . .

The snow had ceased falling; the last of the flakes had fluttered slowly and wearily on to the roofs; and through the dissolving mist the golden sun could be seen tinging the pearly-grey expanse of heaven with a pink glow. Over Montmartre a belt of blue fringed the horizon; but it was so faint and delicate that it seemed but a shadow such as white satin might throw. Paris was gradually detaching itself from amidst the smoke, spreading out more broadly with its snowy expanses the frigid cloak which held it in death-like quiescence. There were now no longer any fleeting specks of white making the city shudder, and quivering in pale waves over the dull-brown housefronts. Amidst the masses of snow that girt them round, the dwellings stood out black and gloomy, as though mouldy with centuries of damp. Entire streets appeared to be in ruins, as if undermined by some gunpowder explosion, with roofs ready to give way and windows already driven in. But gradually, as the belt of blue broadened in the direction of Montmartre, there came a stream of light, pure and cool as the waters of a spring; and Paris once more shone out as under a glass, which lent even to the outlying districts the distinctness of a Japanese picture.

The blue of the heavens was exquisitely clear, but still very pale in the light of the sun, which hung low on the horizon, and glittered like a silver lamp. In that icy temperature its rays shed no heat on the glittering snow. Below stretched the expanse of roofs – the tiles of the Army Bakehouse, and the slates of the houses on the quay – like sheets of white cloth fringed with black. On the other bank of the river, the square stretch of the Champ-de-Mars seemed a steppe, the black dots of the straggling vehicles making one think of sledges skimming along with tinkling bells; while the elms on the Quai d'Orsay, dwarfed by the distance, looked like crystal flowers bristling with sharp points. Through all the snow-white sea the Seine rolled its muddy waters edged by the ermine of its banks; since the evening before ice had been floating down, and you could clearly see the masses crushing against the piers of the Pont des Invalides, and vanishing swiftly beneath the arches. The bridges, growing more and more delicate with the distance, seemed like the steps of a ladder of white lace reaching as far as the sparkling walls of the Cité, above which the towers of Notre-Dame reared their snow-white crests. On the left the level plain was broken up by other peaks. The Church of Saint-Augustin, the Opera House, the Tower of Saint-Jacques, looked like mountains clad with eternal snow. Nearer at hand the pavilions of the Tuileries and the Louvre, joined together by newly erected buildings, resembled a ridge of hills with spotless summits. On the right, too, were the white tops of the Invalides, of Saint-Sulpice, and the Panthéon, the last in the dim distance, outlining against the sky a palace of fairyland with dressings of bluish marble. Not a sound broke the stillness. Grey-looking hollows revealed the presence of the streets; the public squares were like yawning crevasses. Whole lines of houses had vanished. The fronts of the neighboring dwellings alone showed distinctly with the thousand streaks of light reflected from their windows. Beyond, the expanse of snow intermingled and merged into a seeming lake, whose blue shadows blended with the blue of the sky. Huge and clear in the bright, frosty atmosphere, Paris glittered in the light of the silver sun.

Zola himself had foreseen that his new novel would not satisfy his readers; that is exactly what happened. Written partly in the suburbs of Marseille, *A Love Episode,* published in 1878, after *The Dram-shop,* disappointed its readers. Their appetite whetted, these readers demanded that the experimental novelist supply them with stronger nourishment.

But Zola, who at times still felt some nostalgia when he thought of Musset, had wanted to show that his palette included delicate colors. It cost him a mediocre book and a decrease in sales.

It was then that Edmond de Goncourt saw him, Zola's eyes dull behind his pince-nez, disillusioned, whining, speaking bitterly: one of the novels in the series was stuck. Success was necessary for Zola, an immediate, a resounding success; as soon as the last line was written, the galley proofs corrected, he became the publicity chief all over again. He followed the sales curve passionately. It was his temperature graph. If the line went up, he was lively, happy, the world seemed bright to him, the experimental novel was the last word in science; if the sales stagnated, he whined for a few days, then dreamed of revenge, imagining new ways of taking his public in hand again. If the public wanted scandals, it would have them, for Zola knew none of the anxieties which sometimes get the better of a writer after a success and make him fear to disappoint his readers with the books that will follow.

His golden rule, the motto which he gave his friends and his disciples was: "Let us write a lot." Nothing exasperates him more than a young writer who confides to him his doubts about the novel he is writing. He never feels more confident than after a successful book. "Forge ahead," he advises. He is a man of action. The two towers at Médan are built of something other than ivory; their windows open on the whole world. Zola has a panoramic view from his fortress; peering through the battlements, he watches from behind his pince-nez.

Though for a moment he sought to baffle his readers, in doing so, he did not lose his sense of reality. He writes to Mme. Charpentier:

> We must resign ourselves to the fact that we will not repeat the success of *The Dram-shop*. This time, *A Love Episode* (I am satisfied with that title since it is the best of all those I have found) is a work too tender to take the public by storm. We need not have any illusions on that score. Let us sell ten thousand copies and consider ourselves satisfied. But we will make up with *Nana*. I am dreaming now of an extraordinary *Nana*. You will see. This time it will really be murder for Charpentier and myself.

LA LUNE
ROUSSE

LA NAISSANCE DE NANA-VÉNUS — PAR GILL

Motif à tableau pour les BOUGUEREAU futurs.

Paul Alexis

Huysmans   Guy de Maupassant

Émile Zola

Léon Hennique   Henry Céard

Nana

About this time, between 1877 and 1880, a group of writers, younger than he by a few years, had formed the habit of calling on Émile Zola at his house in Médan. The most faithful were Huysmans, Guy de Maupassant, Henri Céard, Léon Hennique, and Paul Alexis. Of course, they all claimed to be part of the naturalistic school. Out of these meetings a book was to appear in 1880: *Evenings at Médan (Les Soirées de Médan)*, containing a short story by each of these six writers. Zola's story was entitled *The Attack on the Mill (L'Attaque de Moulin)*; Maupassant's story, *Ball of Fat (Boule de Suif)*, was to make its author famous at the age of thirty.

Since *A Love Episode* has been a failure, Zola prepares his revenge. This time he will describe the life of a courtesan. Unfortunately, he is chaste, as he likes to say; this is a milieu of society which he does not know well. Again he draws on his friends' experience; Goncourt, Daudet, Céard, and others help him with their advice, introduce him to the social lionesses. He writes to Céard:

> Thank you very much for your notes. They are excellent, and I shall use all of them; the dinner especially is astound-

ing. I should like to have a hundred pages of notes like these. I should then write a very good book. If you find any more, by yourself or through your friends, send me another package. I am starved for the real thing.

I have in mind the plan for *Nana*, and I am very happy. It took me three days to find the names, some of which seem to me very good; I must tell you that I already have sixty characters. I shall not be able to begin writing for two more weeks, because I still have so many details to take care of.

August 9, 1878, he announces to Flaubert:

I have just finished the plan for *Nana*; it gave me a lot of trouble because it deals with a singularly complex world, and I shall have no less than a hundred characters. I am very happy with this plan. However, I think that it will be quite stiff. I want to say everything, and some of it is quite coarse. You will be satisfied, I think, with the paternal and bourgeois fashion in which I am going to treat the good "*filles de joie*."
... In my pen at this moment I feel that little tremor that always has augured the happy birth of a good book.... I expect to begin writing about the twentieth of this month, after my Russian correspondence.

Zola was right to feel happy. Without reaching the breadth of *The Dram-shop* or later of *Germinal* this novel is one of the best of the series.

Here is what Flaubert will write about it to Charpentier: "What a book! What a blow! And the good Zola is a genius, hear ye, hear ye!"

Then to the author himself:

If I had to make a note of everything rare and powerful in it, I should have to make a comment at every page! The characters are marvelously true. Plain words abound in it; at the end Nana's death is *Michaelangelesque!*

A most powerful book, old man!

... Now, you may have been thrifty with the coarse words, I believe it! The ordinary fare of the lesbians may shock "all sense of decency," it's possible! Well! What of it! To hell with the idiots. It is original, in any case, and swaggeringly done.

The word "Mignon," what a tool! And the whole character of "Mignon," as a matter of fact, delights me.

Nana turns to myth, without ceasing to be real.

The novel opens with the somewhat photographic pages describing the evening during which the daughter of Gervaise and Coupeau makes her stage debut; it is a bit of boldness, the high C of the experimental novel. But the author is soon caught in his own game; evidently he likes Nana, and he would enjoy being in Fontan's place.

Once more Zola competes with the master painters. He will be Rubens, Courbet, Renoir. Nana is plump and blond, her flesh is glorious, her chest is like a young Amazon's, and the more intimate parts of her body are not always immaculate, as is fitting in a naturalistic novel. Zola shows her to us in all her various aspects; naughty in her dressing room during the royal prince's visit, a shirt tail hanging all the while out of her drawers, as she comes and goes among her admirers and applies her make-up, with her breast bare; then on stage, after a scene where she appears in tights, bowing as she walks backwards, leaning forward, her hips flaring out. Then, proceeding gradually, Zola lets us see her naked, warming herself by an open fire, admiring herself as she holds her breasts in both hands.

Those descriptions are beautiful; the theoretician of the experimental novel is all excited, he does not tire of painting his model; he becomes sentimental; he turns Nana into a good girl who ruins men without thinking, as she would munch an apple. Weak also, naturally, falling in love with a dreadful dance-hall clown who beats her, for Nana likes that, of course. The scientific novel catches fire in these pages, but it is no laboratory flame that caresses Nana's golden flesh. The chaste Émile Zola makes up for lost time. We have come a long way since *Madame Bovary*.

First of all, here is Nana's debut on the stage:

> At that very moment the clouds at the back of the stage were cloven apart, and Venus appeared. Exceedingly tall, exceedingly strong for her eighteen years, Nana, in her goddess's white tunic, and with her light hair simply flowing unfastened over her shoulders, came down to the footlights, with a quiet certainty of movement, and a laugh of greeting for the public, and struck up her grand ditty, –
>
> "When Venus roams at eventide."
>
> From the second verse onward, people looked at each other

all over the house. Was this some jest, some wager on Bordenave's part? Never had a more tuneless voice been heard, or one managed with less art. Her manager judged of her excellently; she certainly sang like a squirt. Nay, more, she didn't even know how to deport herself on the stage: she thrust her arms in front of her, while she swayed her whole body to and fro in a manner which struck the audience as unbecoming and disagreeable. Cries of "Oh, Oh!" were already rising in the pit and the cheap places. There was a sound of whistling too, when a voice in the stalls, suggestive of a moulting cockerel, cried out with great conviction, – "That's very smart!"

All the house looked round. It was the cherub, the truant from the boarding-school, who sat with his fine eyes very wide open, and his fair face glowing very hotly at sight of Nana. When he saw everybody turning towards him, he grew extremely red at the thought of having thus unconsciously spoken aloud. Daguenet, his neighbour, smilingly examined him; the public laughed, as though disarmed, and no longer anxious to hiss; while the young gentlemen in white gloves, fascinated in their turn by Nana's gracious contours, lolled back in their seats and applauded.

"That's it! well done! Bravo!"

Nana, in the mean time, seeing the house laughing, began to laugh herself. The gaiety of all redoubled itself. She was an amusing creature, all the same, was that fine girl! Her laughter made a love of a little dimple appear in her chin. She stood there waiting, not bored in the least, familiar with her audience, falling into step with them at once, as though she herself were admitting, with a wink, that she had not two farthings' worth of talent, but that it did not matter at all, that in fact she had other good points. And then, after having made a sign to the conductor which plainly signified, "Go ahead, old boy!" she began her second verse: –

"Tis Venus who at midnight passes – –"

Still the same acidulated voice, only that now it tickled the public in the right quarter so deftly that momentarily it caused them to give a little shiver of pleasure. Nana still smiled her smile: it lit up her little red mouth, and shone in her great eyes, which were of the clearest blue. When she came to certain rather lively verses, a delicate sense of enjoyment made her tilt her nose, the rosy nostrils of which lifted and fell, while a bright flush suffused her cheeks. She still swung herself up and down, for she only knew how to do that. And the trick was no longer voted ugly; on the contrary, the men raised their opera-glasses. When she came to the end of a verse, her voice completely failed her, and she was well aware that she never would get through with it. Thereupon, rather than fret herself, she kicked up her leg, which forthwith was roundly outlined under her diaphanous tunic, bent sharply backwards, so that her bosom was thrown upward and forward, and stretched her arms out. Applause burst forth on all sides. In the twinkling of an eye she had turned on her heel, and was going up the stage, presenting the nape of her neck to the spectators' gaze, a neck where the red gold hair shewed like some animal's fell. Then the plaudits became frantic.

Let us look at the second tableau. Nana's dressing room is invaded by admirers during the intermission.

"I beg your pardon, gentlemen," said Nana, drawing aside the curtain, "but you took me by surprise."

They all turned round. She had not clothed herself at all, had in fact only buttoned on a little pair of linen stays which half revealed her bosom. When the gentlemen had put her to flight, she had scarcely begun undressing, and was rapidly taking off her fish-wife's costume. Through the opening in her drawers behind, a corner of her shift was even now visible. There she stood, bare-armed, bare-shouldered, bare-breasted, in all the adorable glory of her youth and plump fair beauty, but she still held the curtain with one hand, as though ready to draw it to again upon the slightest provocation.

"Yes, you took me by surprise! I never shall dare – –" she stammered in pretty mock confusion, while rosy blushes crossed her neck and shoulders, and smiles of embarassment played about her lips.

"Oh, don't apologize," cried Bordenave, "since these gentlemen approve of your good looks!"

But she still tried the hesitating, innocent, girlish game, and, shivering as though someone were tickling her, she continued:

"His highness does me too great an honour. I beg his highness will excuse my receiving him thus – –"

"It is I who am importunate," said the Prince, "but, madam, I could not resist the desire of complimenting you."

Thereupon, in order to reach her dressing-table, she walked very quietly, and just as she was, through the midst of the gentlemen, who made way for her to pass.

She had strongly-marked hips, which filled her drawers out roundly, whilst, with swelling bosom, she still continued bowing, and smiling her delicate little smile. Suddenly she seemed to recognise Count Muffat, and she extended her hand to him as an old friend. Then she scolded him for not having come to her supper-party. His highness deigned to chaff Muffat about this, and the latter stammered and thrilled again at the thought that, for one second, he had held in his own feverish clasp a little fresh and perfumed hand. The Count had dined excellently at the Prince's, who indeed was a heroic eater and drinker. Both of them were even a little intoxicated, but they behaved very creditably. To hide the commotion within him, Muffat could only remark about the heat.

"Good Heavens, how hot it is here!" said he. "How do you manage to live in such a temperature, madam?"

And here is the crowning-piece:

One of Nana's pleasures consisted in undressing herself in front of the mirror on her wardrobe door, which reflected her whole height. She would let everything slip off her in turn, and then would stand perfectly naked, and gaze and gaze in complete oblivion of all around her. Passion for her own body, ecstasy over her satin skin and the supple contours of her shape, would keep her serious, attentive, and absorbed in the love of herself. The hair-dresser frequently found her standing thus, and would enter without her once turning to look at him. Muffat used to grow angry then, but he only succeeded in astonishing her. What was coming over the man? She was doing it to please herself, not other people.

That particular evening, she wanted to have a better view of herself, and she lit the six candles attached to the frame of the mirror. But while letting her shift slip down, she paused. She had been preoccupied for some moments past and a question was on her lips.

"You haven't read the *Figaro* article, have you? The paper's on the table."

Daguenet's laugh had recurred to her recollection, and she was harassed by a doubt. If that Fauchery had slandered her, she would be revenged.

"They say that it's about me," she continued, affecting indifference. "What's your notion, eh, darling?"

And letting go her shift, and waiting till Muffat should have done reading, she stood naked. Muffat was reading slowly Fauchery's article, entitled "The Golden Fly," describing the life of a harlot, descended from four or five generations of drunkards, and tainted in her blood by a cumulative inheritance of misery and drink, which in her case has taken the form of a nervous exaggeration of the sexual instinct. She has shot up to womanhood in the slums and on the pavements of Paris and tall, handsome, and as superbly grown as a dunghill plant, she avenges the beggars and outcasts of whom she is the ultimate product. With her the rottenness that is allowed to ferment among the populace is carried upwards and rots the aristocracy. She becomes a blind power of nature, a leaven of destruction, and unwittingly she corrupts and disorganises all Paris, churning it between her snow-white thighs as milk is monthly churned by housewives. And it was at the end of this article that the comparison with a fly occurred, a fly of sunny hue, which has flown up out of the dung, a fly which sucks in death on the carrion tolerated by the roadside, and then buzzing, dancing, and glittering like a precious stone, enters the windows of palaces and poisons the men within by merely settling on them in her flight.

Muffat lifted his head; his eyes stared fixedly; he gazed at the fire.

"Well?" asked Nana.

But he did not answer. It seemed as though he wanted to read the article again. A cold shivering feeling was creeping from his scalp to his shoulders. This article had been written anyhow. The phrases were wildly extravagant, the unexpected epigrams and quaint collections of words went beyond all bounds. Yet, notwithstanding this, he was struck by what he had read, for it had rudely awakened within him much that for months past he had not cared to think about.

He looked up. Nana had grown absorbed in her ecstatic

ZOLA, BY MANET

NANA, BY MANET

While it is certain that the painter was not inspired by the novel, and probable that the novelist was not inspired by the painting, it is possible that each had the same model in mind. Manet's model, in any case, was the actress Henriette Hauser, nicknamed "Lemon" ("Citron") (Hamburg, Kunsthalle, No. 2376)

self-contemplation. She was bending her neck and was looking attentively in the mirror at a little brown mark above her right haunch. She was touching it with the tip of her finger, and by dint of bending backward was making it stand out more clearly than ever. Situated where it was, it doubtless struck her as both quaint and pretty. After that she studied other parts of her body with an amused expression, and much of the vicious curiosity of a child. The sight of herself always astonished her, and she would look as surprised and ecstatic as a young girl who has discovered her puberty. Slowly, slowly she spread out her arms in order to give full value to her figure, which suggested the torso of a plump Venus. She bent herself this way and that, and examined herself before and behind, stopping to look at the side-view of her bosom and at the sweeping contours of her thighs. And she ended with a strange amusement, which consisted of swinging to right and left, her knees apart, and her body swaying from the waist with the perpetual jogging, twitching movements peculiar to an Oriental dancer in the *danse du ventre*.

Muffat sat looking at her. She frightened him. The newspaper had dropped from his hand. For a moment he saw her as she was, and he despised himself. Yes, it was just that; she had corrupted his life, he already felt himself tainted to his very marrow by impurities hitherto undreamt of. Everything was now destined to rot within him, and in the twinkling of an eye he understood what this evil entailed. He saw the ruin brought about by this kind of "leaven" – himself poisoned, his family destroyed, a bit of the social fabric cracking and crumbling. And, unable to take his eyes from the sight, he sat looking fixedly at her, striving to inspire himself with loathing for her nakedness.

Nana no longer moved. With an arm behind her neck, one hand clasped in the other, and her elbows far apart, she was throwing back her head, so that he could see a foreshortened reflection of her half-closed eyes, her parted lips, her face clothed with amorous laughter. Her masses of yellow hair were unknotted behind, and they covered her back with the fell of a lioness.

Bending back thus, she displayed her solid Amazonian waist and firm bosom, where strong muscles moved under the satin texture of the skin. A delicate line, to which the shoulder and the thigh added their slight undulations, ran from one of her elbows to her foot, and Muffat's eyes followed this tender profile, and marked how the outlines of the fair flesh vanished in golden gleams, and how its rounded contours shone like silk in the candle-light. He thought of his old dread of Woman, of the Beast of the Scriptures, at once lewd and wild. Nana was all covered with fine hair, a russet down made her body velvety; whilst the Beast was apparent in the almost equine development of her flanks, in the fleshy exuberances and deep hollows of her body, which lent her sex the mystery and suggestiveness lurking in their shadows. She was, indeed that Golden Creature, blind as brute force, whose very odour ruined the world. Muffat gazed and gazed as a man possessed, till, at last, when he had shut his eyes in order to escape it, the Brute reappeared in the darkness of the brain, larger, more terrible, more suggestive in its attitude. Now, he understood, it would remain before his eyes, in his very flesh, forever.

But Nana was gathering herself together. A little thrill of tenderness seemed to have traversed her members. Her eyes were moist; she tried, as it were, to make herself small, as though she could feel herself better thus. Then she threw her head and bosom back, and melting, as it were, in one great bodily caress, she rubbed her cheeks coaxingly first against one shoulder then against the other. Her lustful mouth breathed desire over her limbs. She put out her lips, kissed herself long and long in the neighbourhood of her armpit, and laughed at the other Nana who, also, was kissing herself in the mirror.

Then Muffat gave a long sigh. This solitary pleasure exasperated him. Suddenly all his resolutions were swept away as though by a mighty wind. In a fit of brutal passion he caught Nana to his breast and threw her down on the carpet.

If the theory of heredity is subtracted from Zola's work, and it could be done with little harm, his construction appears rigorously similar to Balzac's. In both of them there is the same reciprocal movement which carries characters from one book to the next, with a weaver's motion. The plot, beyond each novel, attempts to cover the whole work with its net, but often, it is true, in an external manner: that is, as an author's convenience rather than a strict necessity.

We know that Nana is Gervaise's daughter because Zola tells us so, but we cannot see that it adds much to the book or to the character. From time to time we are reminded that the girl is the same girl we met in *The Dram-shop*, but those reminders of the past are so foreign to the very story we are reading that they hardly make any impression on us. Nana never meets any of her former shop-mates, nor anyone she used to know except her aunt. Not once does she go by the neighborhood where she lived as a child. Nothing can indicate better how artificial the method is, for such a break with the past – almost complete – seems inconceivable.

As soon as it was published, *Nana* was a huge success; the choice of subject, the real characters which seemed to appear behind the fictional ones contributed to it a great deal. Scandal was not the least important factor of success. The attacks against Zola redoubled. Those who had applauded *The Dramshop* because the shame of the working classes was exposed in it, hissed *Nana* which unveiled the weaknesses of self-righteous circles.

Zola, enchanted, listens to the tumult, and answers the accusations of obscenity with his eternal arguments: he is a good bourgeois, without vices, without passions. He describes life, he shows what he sees, what he knows; he could give a hundred examples – taken from real life – of what he advances in his books; besides, everybody knows it, including those who scream the loudest. On what grounds could he be forbidden to speak of what really exists? He makes a distinction, as a matter of fact, between the writers who can justly be called erotic, those who intend only to flatter the worst instincts of their readers, and himself who, seeking inspiration in truth alone, intends solely to moralize.

Judging from the numbers who read *Nana*, those who wished to reform must have been many....

Actually Zola's only test is reality. It is reality, and only reality which can justify the writer in his opinion. Is what you say real? Have you lived it, observed it, have trustworthy people seen it? If so, no moral law can forbid you to make it the subject of your book, however scandalous it may appear. For a doctor there are no shameful diseases; for the novelist no passions of which he should refrain from speaking; he has the right – better still, the duty – to write about them. That is why

Zola will write the preface to a homosexual's journal, although the book was anonymous. That is why also he will condemn in the strongest fashion the Marquis de Sade, using almost word for word the criticisms leveled against himself. In that author's works, as well as in *Le Maudit* by a certain Abbé X., he sees only imaginary monstrosities, caricatures of reality, the works of maniacs.

He forbids the novelist's imagination to smudge wantonly the human condition, but he thinks that a moral ideal can always be derived from real facts, however horrible, and that the remedy is always found next to the evil. In short, he is profoundly moralistic.

And the factor that contributes so much to his confidence is the certainty he has of being a virtuous man himself; and it is true: he is temperate, modest, truthful, faithful to his friends. Thus armed from head to toe with virtue, he can explore all the weakness and all the baseness of man without ever feeling involved in them. He has the fortitude of the surgeon in the operating room. Besides, he has the highest possible opinion of his art, and nothing will ever be able to divert him from what appears to him to be the truth. This will certainly be evident during the Dreyfus affair.

Nana is still making a devil of a noise when Zola starts doing research again. This time, it is for *The Boarding House (Pot-Bouille)*.

On June 6, 1881, he writes Huysmans:

> Thank you for your valuable information; I must again trouble you with more precise questions.
>
> My architect, who is not very important, lives in Paris, probably rue de Choiseul, and he happens to be a member of the Saint-Roch parish. If I make him the architect of the diocese of Évreux, can I still use him for repairs in the Saint-Roch church? To use him in Paris would probably be to give him an excessively high position. Anyway please find out whether there is a way to do it, whether there are parish architects in Paris, and what their salaries, their responsibilities, etc., would be. But, if I have to confine myself to my diocese of Évreux, please get me more details about the trips to be made, the relations with the clergy, etc. However, I would greatly prefer Paris.

Just as he had done for *A Love Episode,* Zola works at *The*

Boarding House with his usual steadfastness, but without much dash. That is what he writes Henry Céard on August 24, 1881:

> I always work in a stable atmosphere. No mistake about it, my novel is a work of precision and neatness. No heroic tone, not a single lyrical feast. I don't get any great satisfaction from it, but it amuses me like a machine with a thousand wheels which it is my job to regulate with meticulous care. I ask myself this question: When we think we have a passion, is it really so clever to reject it or even to restrain it? If one of my books endures, it will certainly be the most passionate one. Well, we must vary our tune and try everything. All this is simply an academic question; for I repeat that I am very satisfied with *The Boarding House* which I call my *Sentimental Education*.

The Boarding House is an extremely long book, and unfortunately it seems so. One of its weaknesses is the fact that it is a sort of caricature of naturalism because it contains too many of the clichés of the school. In spite of some successful pages, especially those which show Berthe caught with her lover in the middle of the night, this novel seems monotonous.

All the characters are tenants of the same building, and the story is an endless imbroglio of intrigues. Perhaps the greatest weakness of *The Boarding House* is the fact that it really contains a dozen novels; another weakness lies in the characters: the author wanted them to be mediocre, and he can't quite succeed in interesting us in the life of this lower middle class.

Zola put himself in a corner of the picture; he has one of his characters say that his lewd novels are worth their weight in gold on the market. It is very probable that the tenants of a house where he lived in Paris served as models, with the usual naturalistic arrangements – which does not suit them.

André Gide, however, liked the work; he put down in his *Journal*:

> I have just re-read *The Boarding House* with admiration. Oh, to be sure, I recognize Zola's shortcomings; but, just like those of Balzac or so many others, they cannot be divorced from his qualities; and the brutality, the strength of his pictures is devoid of delicacy or subtlety. It is the excess itself in *The Boarding House* which I like, and its perseverance in the filth and the odious. Octave and Berthe's rendezvous in the maid's room and the defiling of their miserable love under the

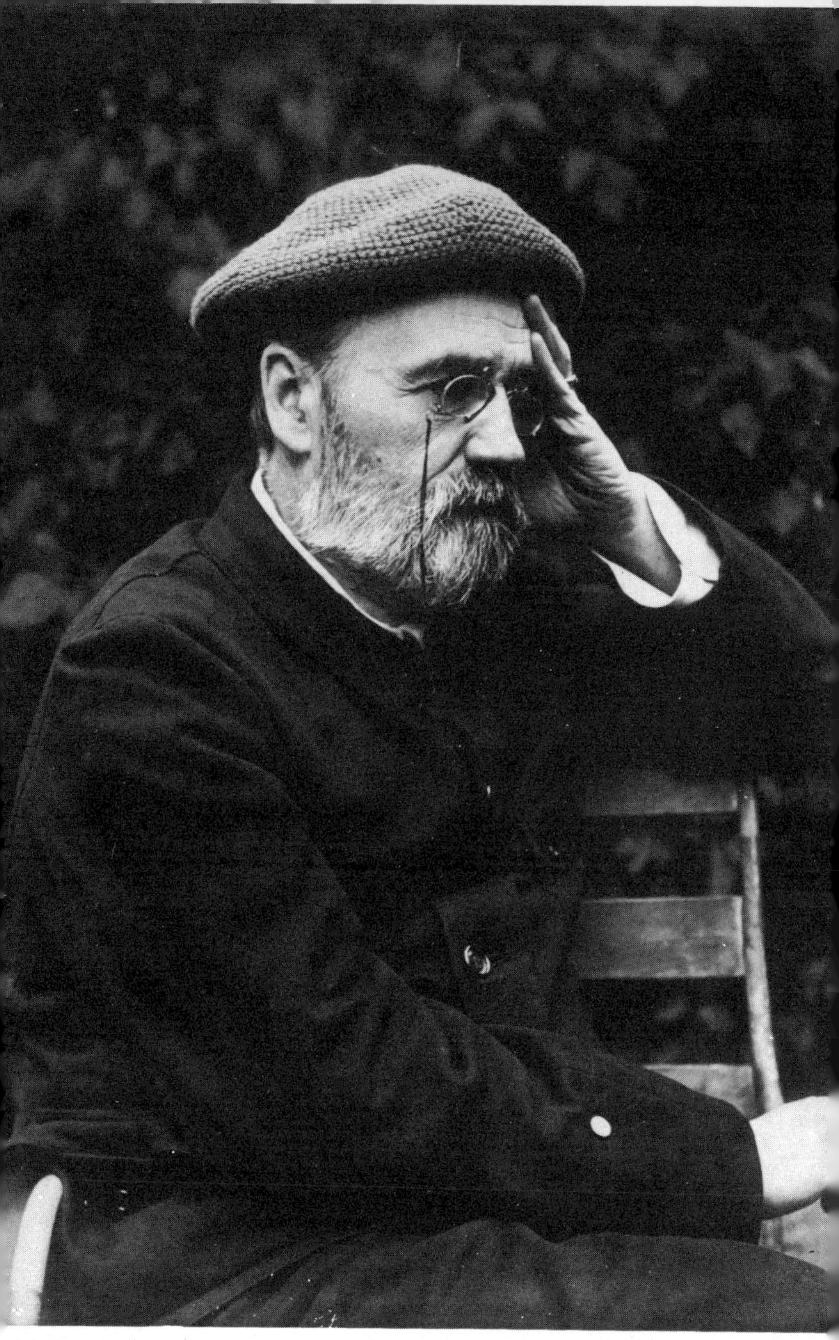

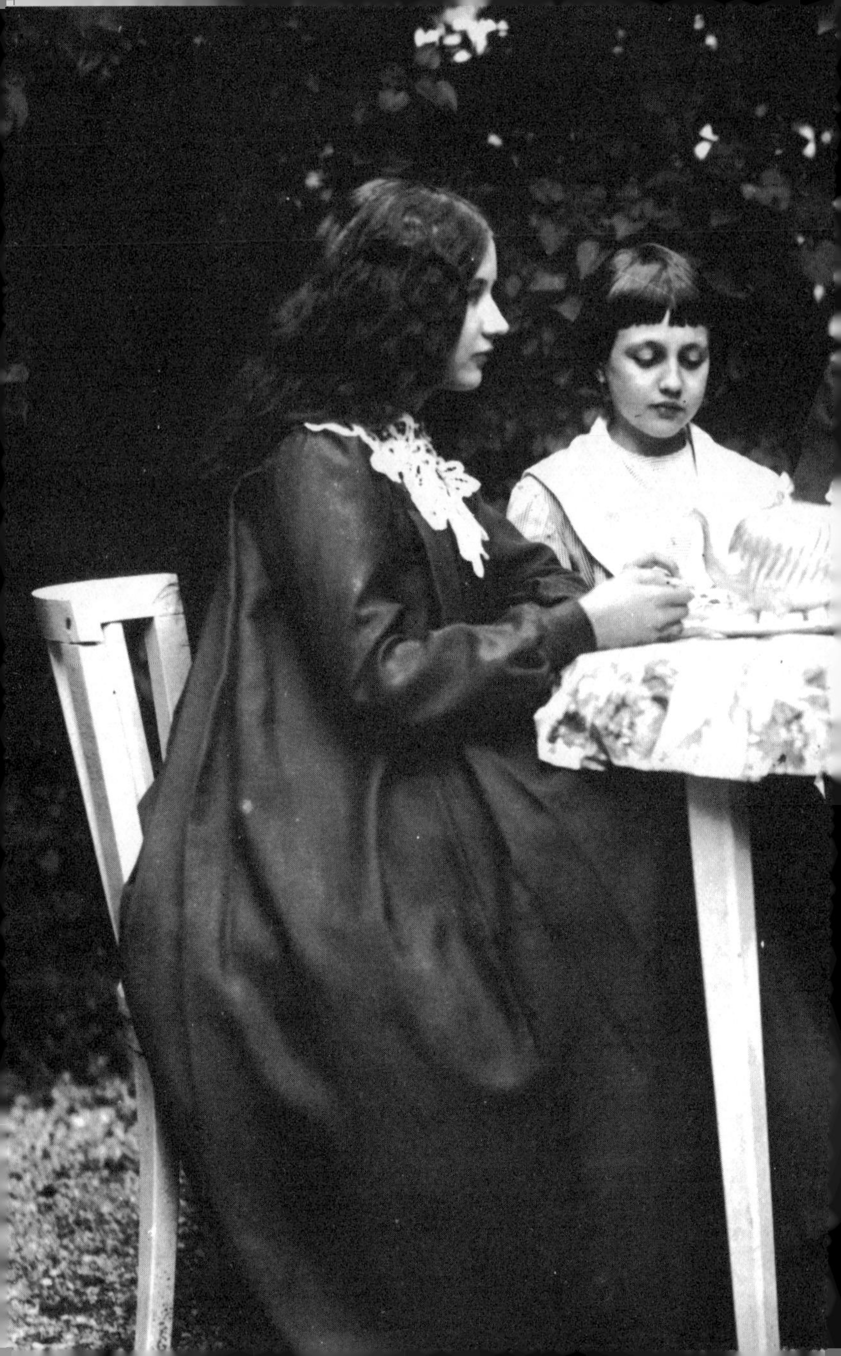

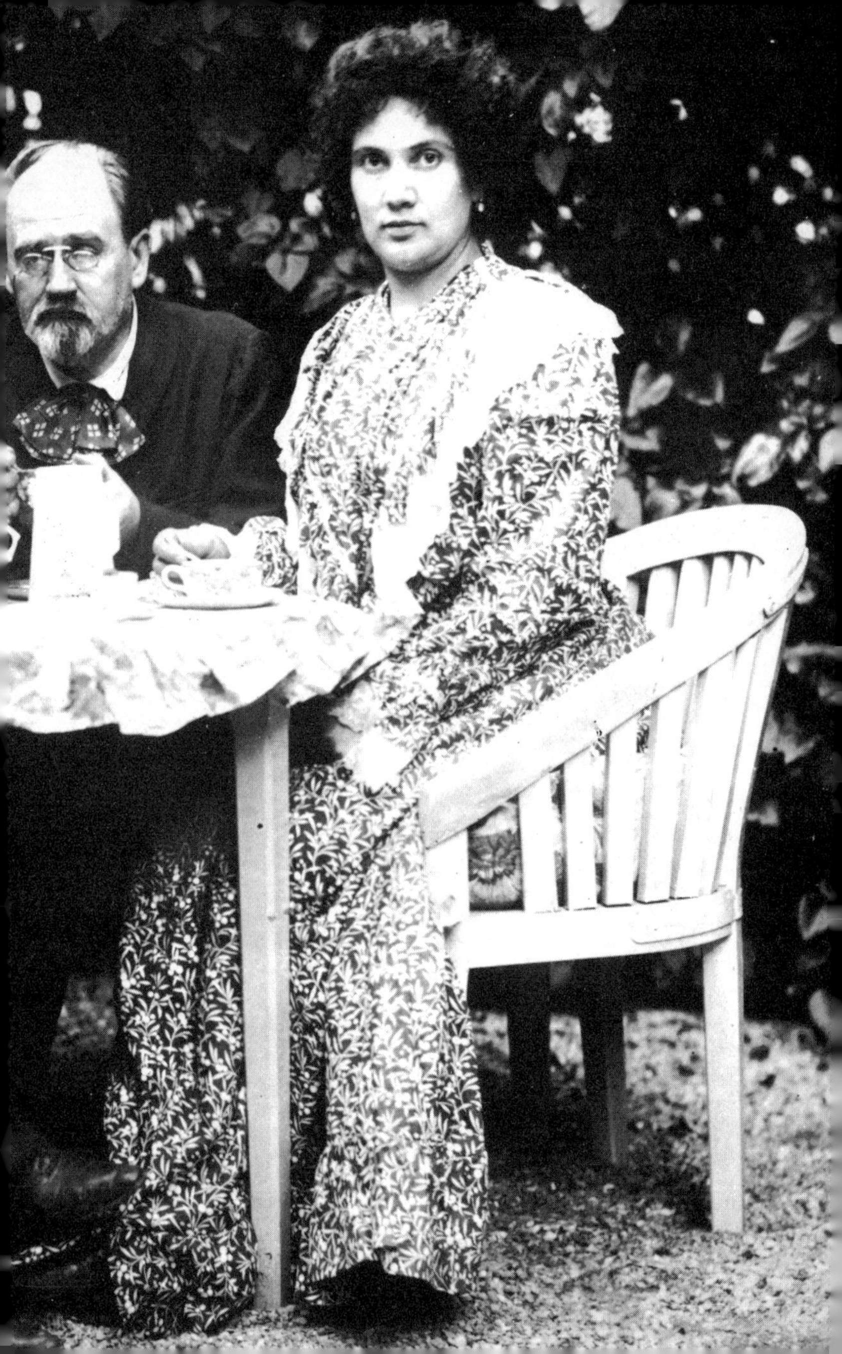

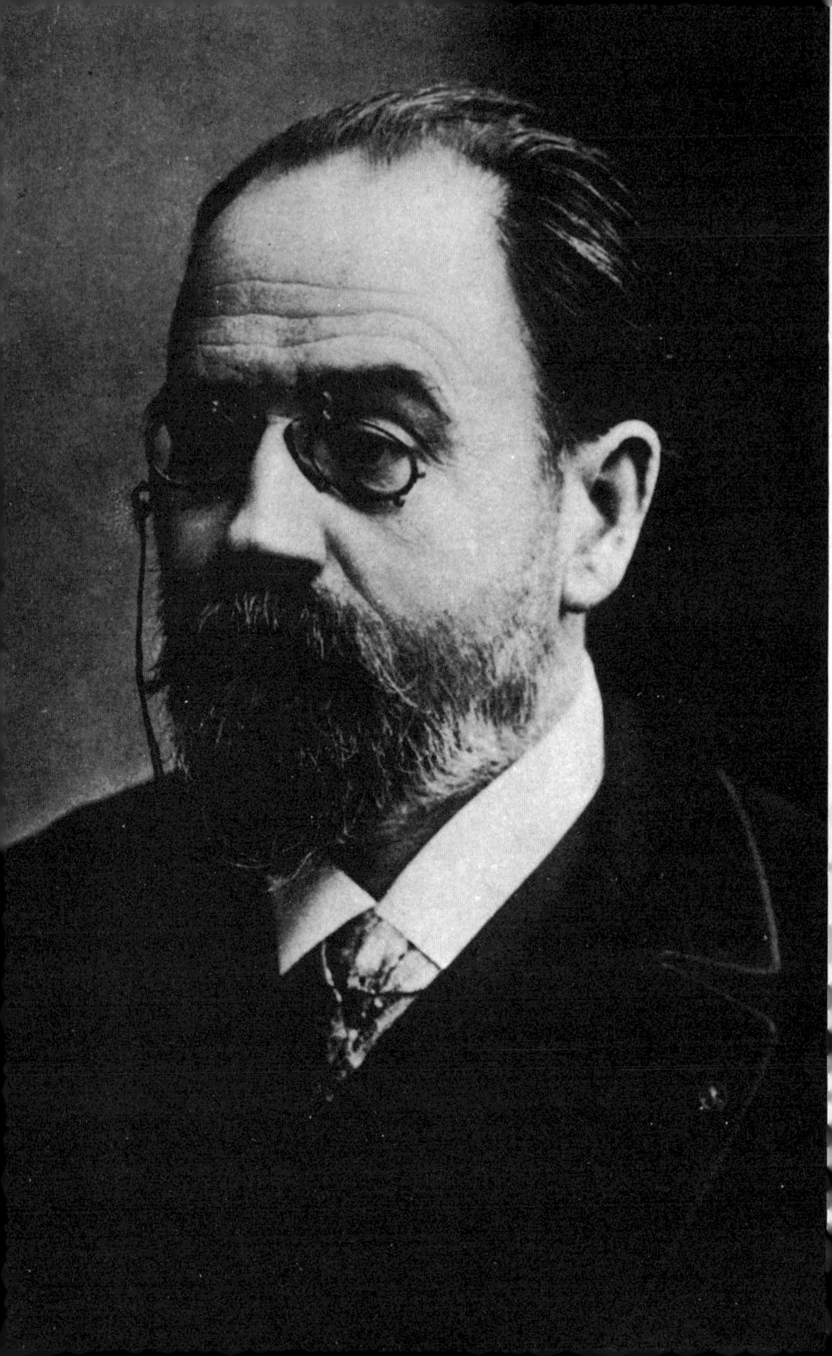

foul flow of the servants' language, Adèle's clandestine accouchement, the family scenes, Mme. Josserand's and her daughters' explanations (a little too often repeated, as are almost all the effects in this book) are drawn by a masterful hand and cannot be forgotten. The characters are excessively simplified, but they are not puppets, and their picturesque conversations have an accuracy of tone which is quite rare in Balzac. I consider Zola's present disrepute as a monstrous injustice which does not enhance the credit of our contemporary literary critics. There is not a more personal nor more representative French novelist.

This praise is not as surprising as it may seem. André Gide liked to repeat that he was attracted most by what was farthest from him; there is in Zola's virile talent a power that must have subdued him.

ZOLA IN THE CITY AND ZOLA IN THE COUNTRY
(with Pinpin, a Pomeranian dog)

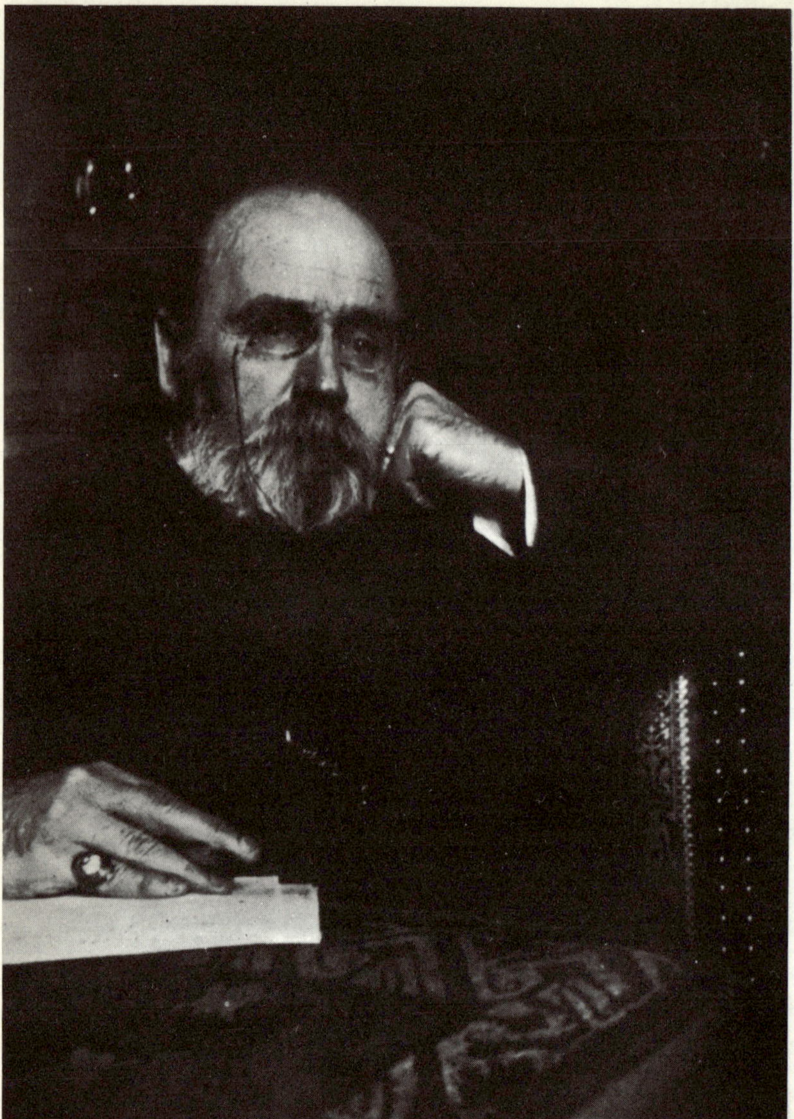

*The Ladies' Paradise** (Au bonheur des dames)*

During the two years following the publication of *The Boarding House*, two other novels of the series appear: *The Ladies' Paradise* (1883), and *The Joy of Life* (1884). Both belong among his more mediocre works, but the first is interesting because of Zola's preoccupations which take him beyond everyday morals.

The Dram-Shop was still considered a simple denunciation of drunkenness in the working classes, and everybody could subscribe to its views, which did not go much beyond the temperance campaigns. *The Ladies' Paradise* shows that Zola had a deeper interest in the economic questions of the day; he had read Fourier, Guesde, Proudhon, and Marx. He is attracted by socialism; its doctrine might well lure him since it tends to treat man in the mass, as he does; it also plays down individual values, and it believes in infinite progress, in science and technology.

Although Zola denied for a long time that his writings had any partisan tendencies, his whole personality and his conception of the world were almost inevitably to bring him closer to socialism. This did not happen without some arguments, as his controversy with Proudhon proves.

In *The Ladies' Paradise*, the struggle between the large commercial firms and the small tradespeople is a constantly underlying thesis, a thought that runs through the book. But Zola is still too concerned about his art to let the thesis encumber and subjugate the story – as will happen later when, in the works of his last years, the prophet will take precedence over the novelist. For the time being, truth is enough for him. To show what he sees, how he sees it, to spare nothing and nobody – such is his intention.

An atheist, a positivist, having known poverty for many years, not afraid to show the seamy aspects of life, Zola was to be the first novelist to feel the inevitable arrival of economic determinism. In his book, the coming of the corporations is around the corner, the department stores loom on the horizon in a flood of lights, while all around, in the dark and deserted little shops, the small merchants are desperate.

The main character of the book is the store, managed by Mouret, who is from the south of France. Zola does not tire of describing it in all its aspects, in his usual epic manner.

* Published in Great Britain as *Ladies Delight*.

Here is the "Ladies' Paradise," on the day of a large sale. A modern adventurer, Mouret takes his greatest risk.

Mouret planted himself alone on the landing of the hall-staircase. From there he commanded the whole shop; around him the departments on the first-floor; beneath, those of the ground-floor. Above, the emptiness seemed heart-breaking; in the lace department, an old woman was having everything turned over and buying nothing; whilst three good-for-nothing minxes in the under-linen department were slowly choosing some collars at eighteen sous. Down below, under the covered galleries, in the ray of light which came in from the street, he noticed that the customers were commencing to get more numerous. It was a slow, broken procession, a promenade before the counters; in the mercery and the haberdashery departments some women of the commoner class were pushing about, but there was hardly a customer in the linen or in the woollen departments. The shop messengers, in their green coats, the buttons of which shone brilliantly, were waiting for customers, their hands dangling about. Now and again there passed an inspector with a ceremonious air, very stiff in his white neck-tie. Mouret was especially grieved by the mortal silence which reigned in the hall, where the light fell from above from a ground glass window, showing a white dust, diffuse and suspended, as it were, under which the silk department seemed to be sleeping, amid a shivering religious silence. A shopman's footstep, a few whispered words, the rustling of a passing skirt, were the only noises heard, and they were almost stifled by the hot air of the heating apparatus. However, carriages began to arrive, the sudden pulling up of the horses was heard, and immediately after the banging of the carriage doors. Outside, a distant tumult was commencing to make itself heard, groups of idlers were pushing in front of the windows, cabs were taking up their positions in the Place Gaillon; there were all the appearances of an approaching crowd. But on seeing the idle cashiers leaning back on their chairs behind their wickets, and observing that the parcel tables with their boxes of string and reams of blue packing-paper remained unoccupied, Mouret, though indignant with himself for being afraid, thought he felt his immense machine stop and turn cold beneath him.

But little by little Mouret regains confidence. Buyers are flocking to the "Ladies' Paradise." Once more the game is won.

Mouret had quitted his post on the stairs some time before. Suddenly he reappeared on the landing of the principal staircase which communicated with the ground floor; and from there he commanded a view of the whole establishment. His face had regained its colour, his faith was restored and increasing before the crowd which was gradually filling the place. It was the expected rush at last, the afternoon crush, which he had for a moment despaired of. All the shopmen were at their posts, a last ring of the bell had announced the end of the third lunch; the disastrous morning, due no doubt to a shower which fell about nine o'clock, could still be repaired, for the blue sky of early morn had resumed its victorious gaiety. Now that the first-floor departments were becoming animated, he was obliged to stand back to make way for the women who were going up to the under-clothing and dress departments; whilst, behind him, in the lace and the shawl departments, he heard large sums bandied about. But the sight of the galleries on the ground-floor especially reassured him. There was a crowd at the haberdashery department, and even the linen and woollen departments were invaded. The procession of buyers closed up, nearly all of a higher class at present, with a few lingering housewives. Under the pale light of the silk hall, ladies had taken off their gloves to feel the Paris Paradise, talking in half-whispers. And there was no longer any mistaking the noises arriving from outside, rolling of cabs, banging of carriage-doors, an increasing tumult in the crowd. He felt the machine commencing to work under him, getting up steam and reviving, from the pay-desks where the money was jingling, and the tables where the messengers were hurriedly packing up the goods, down to the basement, in the delivery-room, which was quickly filling up with the parcels sent down, and the underground rumbling of which seemed to shake the whole house.

. . . .

In the silk department there was also a crowd, the principal crush being opposite the inside display, arranged by Hutin, and to which Mouret had given the finishing touches. It was at the further end of the hall, around one of the small wrought-iron columns which supported the glass roof, a veritable torrent of stuffs, a puffy sheet falling from above and spreading out down to the floor. At first stood out the light satins and tender silks, the satins *à la Reine* and Renaissance, with the pearly tones of spring water; light silks, transparent as crystals – Nile-green, Indian-azure, May-rose, and Danube-blue. Then came the stronger fabrics: marvelous satins, duchess silks, warm tints, rolling in great waves; and right at the bottom, as in a fountain-basin, reposed the heavy stuffs, the figured silks, the damasks, brocades, and lovely silvered silks in the midst of a deep bed of velvet of every sort – black, white, and coloured – skilfully disposed on silk and satin grounds, hollowing out with their medley of colours a still lake in which the reflex of the sky seemed to be dancing. The women, pale with desire, bent over as if to look at themselves. And before this falling cataract they all remained standing, with the secret fear of being carried away by the irruption of such luxury, and with the irresistible desire to jump in amidst it and be lost.

It was no easy matter to get to the staircase. A compact crowd of heads was surging under the galleries, expanding like an overflowing river into the middle of the hall. Quite a battle of business was going on, the salesmen had this population of women at their mercy, passing them from one to the other with feverish haste. The moment of the formidable afternoon rush had arrived, when the over-heated machine led the dance of customers, drawing the money from their very flesh. In the silk department especially a breath of folly seemed to pervade all, the Paris Paradise collected such a crowd that for several minutes Hutin could not advance a step; and Henriette, half-suffocated, having raised her eyes, beheld Mouret at the top of the stairs, his favourite position, from which he could see the victory. She smiled, hoping that he would come down and extricate her. But he did not even recognise her in the crowd; he was still with Vallagnosc, showing him the house, his face beaming with triumph.

The trepidation within was now stifling all outside noise; one no longer heard the rumbling of the vehicles, nor the banging of the carriage-doors; nothing remained above the vast murmur of business but the sentiment of this enormous Paris, of such immensity that it would always furnish buyers.

In the heavy still air, in which the fumes of the heating apparatus warmed the odour of the stuffs, the hubbub increased, made up of all sorts of noises, of the continual walking about, of the same phrases, a hundred times repeated around the counters, of the gold jingling on the brass of the pay-desks, besieged by a legion of purses, and of the baskets on wheels loaded with parcels which were constantly disappearing into the gaping cellars. And, amidst the fine dust, everything finished by getting mixed up, it became impossible to recognise the divisions of the different departments; the haberdashery department over there seemed drowned; further on, in the linen department, a ray of sunshine, entering by the window in the Rue Neuve-Saint-Augustin, was like a golden dart in a heap of snow; close by, in the glove and woollen departments, a dense mass of bonnets and chignons hid the background of the shop from view. The toilettes were no longer visible, the head-dresses alone appeared, decked with feathers and ribbons. A few men's hats introduced here and there a black spot, whilst the women's pale complexions assumed in the fatigue and heat the transparencies of the camellia. At last, Hutin – thanks to his vigorous elbows – was able to open a way for the ladies, by keeping in front of them. But on ascending the stairs, Henriette could not find Mouret, who had just plunged Vallagnosc right into the crowd to complete his bewilderment, himself feeling the physical want of a dip into this bath of success. He lost his breath deliciously, he felt against his limbs a sort of caress from all his customers.

It is near the end of the sale. The "Ladies' Paradise" slowly lets out its crowd of buyers. Mouret, the Napoleon of the drygoods business, looks over the battlefield of his most recent victory.

The crowd was slowly diminishing. The bell, at an hour's interval, had already announced the two first dinners; the third was about to be served, and in the departments there were now only a few lingering customers, whose fever for spending had made them forget the time. Outside nothing was heard but the rolling of the last carriages amidst the husky voice of Paris, the snort of a satiated ogre digesting the linens and cloths, silks and lace, with which he had been gorged since the morning. Inside, beneath the flaming gas-jets, which, burning in the twilight, had lighted up the supreme efforts of the sale, everything appeared like a field of battle still warm with the massacre of the various goods. The salesmen, harassed and fatigued, camped amidst the contents of their shelves and counters, which appeared to have been thrown into the greatest confusion by the furious blast of a hurricane. It was with difficulty that one traversed the galleries on the ground floor, blocked up with a crowd of chairs, and in the glove department it was necessary to step over a pile of cases heaped up around Mignot; in the woollen department there was no means of passing at all, Liénard was dozing on a sea of bales, in which certain piles, still standing, though half destroyed, seemed to be houses that an overflowing river was carrying away; and, further on, the linen department was like a heavy fall of snow, one ran up against icebergs of napkins, and walked on light flakes of handkerchiefs.

The same disorder prevailed upstairs, in the departments of the first floor: the furs were scattered over the flooring, the ready-made clothes were heaped up like the great-coats of wounded soldiers, the lace and the underlinen, unfolded, crumpled, thrown about everywhere, made one think of an army of women who had disrobed there in the disorder of some sudden desire; whilst downstairs, at the other end of the house, the delivery department in full activity was still disgorging the parcels with which it was bursting, and which were carried off by the vans – last vibration of the overheated machine. But it was in the silk department especially, that the customers had flung themselves with the greatest ardour. There they had cleared off everything, there was plenty of room to pass, the hall was bare; the whole of the colossal stock of Paris Paradise had been cut up and carried away, as if by a swarm of devouring locusts. And in the midst of this emptiness, Hutin and Favier were running through the counterfoils of their debit-notes, calculating their commission, still out of breath after the struggle. Favier had made fifteen francs, Hutin had only managed to make thirteen, thoroughly beaten that day, enraged at his bad luck. Their eyes sparkled with the passion for money. The whole shop around them was also adding up figures, glowing with the same fever, in the brutal gaiety of the evening of the battle.

"Well! Bourdoncle," cried out Mouret, "are you trembling still?"

He had returned to his favourite position at the top of the stairs of the first floor, against the balustrade; and, in the presence of the massacre of stuffs which was spread out under him, he indulged in a victorious laugh. His fears of the morning, that moment of unpardonable weakness which nobody would ever know of, inspired him with a greater desire to triumph. The battle was definitely won, the small tradespeople of the neighborhood were done for, and Baron Hartmann was conquered, with his millions and his land. Whilst he was looking at the cashiers bending over their ledgers, adding up long columns of figures, whilst he was listening to the sound of the gold, falling from their fingers into the metal bowls, he already saw the "Ladies' Paradise" growing beyond all bounds, enlarging its hall and prolonging its galleries as far as the Rue du Dix-Décembre.

"And now are you convinced, Bourdoncle," he resumed, "that the house is really too small? We could have sold twice as much."

Bourdoncle humbled himself, enraptured, moreover, to find himself in the wrong. But a new spectacle rendered them grave. As was the custom every evening, Lhomme, the chief cashier, had just collected the receipts from each pay-desk; after having added them up, he usually posted up the total amount after placing the paper on which it was written on his file. He then took the receipts up to the chief cashier's office, in a leather case and in bags, according to the nature of the cash. On this occasion the gold and silver predominated, and he was slowly walking upstairs, carrying three enormous bags. Deprived of his right arm, cut off at the elbow, he clasped them in this left arm against his breast, holding one up with his chin to prevent it slipping. His heavy breathing could be heard at a distance, he passed along, staggering and superb, amidst the respectful shopmen.

"How much, Lhomme?" asked Mouret.

"Eighty thousand seven hundred and forty-two francs two sous," replied the cashier.

A joyous laugh stirred up the "Ladies' Paradise." The amount ran through the establishment. It was the highest figure ever attained in one day by a draper's shop.

octobre 83.

Mon cher ami,

Vous serez bien aimable de ne pas parler du tout à Zola de ce que je vous ai lu de mon Cédipine. Je vois dans l'annonce du Gil Blas, qu'on trouvera dans son livre une figure de jeune fille d'une belle vaillance dans le combat à la vie. Donc c'est une jeune fille qu'il est en train de fabriquer et comme il a l'habitude de s'assimiler inconsciemment ce qu'il entend lire au-delà, je ne voudrais pas, moi qui paraîtrai après lui, avoir l'air de l'avoir plagié.

Amitiés
Edmond de Goncourt

Edmond de Goncourt to Henry Céard

Germinal

With *Germinal* Zola shows best the extent to which he was prepared to understand the socialist gospel, for with it he comes in direct contact with the industrial proletariat, and he goes to the heart of the workers' condition. Consequently, he prepares this book with great care; he is no longer satisfied with a hurried investigation, as he was for some of his novels, but he goes to live for several months in a mining district. He lives in the miners' housing developments, drinks beer and gin in the taverns, goes down into a pit, observes his model at work, attends the auctioning of the coal veins, and sees the miners, thrown into competition by the Company, lower the price of a load of coal cent by cent, because they are afraid of unemployment.

He familiarizes himself with the miners' little houses, whose walls are so thin that they let in every noise from neighboring families. He learns about diseases incurred in the mine, about wages, methods of mining; he learns how to prop a gallery, how to push the little coal trucks; he watches the miners squatting in the vein, while coal dust fills the air and water seeps down the walls. For the first time he gauges human suffering.

Here again Zola is original – he mixes journalism with fiction. His hero is a union. Indeed, beyond the group of characters in the foreground, the real hero of *Germinal* is the crowd of miners: it fills the pages, gives the book power and stature. The chorus of ancient tragedy reappears in the most modern of novels; it recaptures the importance it had in Aeschylus' work.

Perhaps it has not been said often enough how much Zola's methods, his visual perception, his way of thinking in pictorial terms liken him to a stage or screen director and make most of his novels resemble films. For *Germinal* he uses a triple screen.

Here again, Émile Zola will avoid idealizing his model; he will let the facts speak for themselves. Opposite the workers, he poses the engineers, a stockholder, the owner of a small mine, but with the same lack of bias. Nothing is less like a propaganda work than *Germinal*, and this adds to its persuasiveness, for it is sufficient to show the condition of the working man of that time to shake our consciences. *Germinal* is the Dreyfus affair of the working class.

As soon as he conceives the project, Émile Zola knows the size of his subject; the immensity of the task does not frighten him because his method of work has proven itself. As the civil-servant of literature that he is, he will assemble his material; as an artist he will breathe into it the breath of life.

The subject matter of *Germinal* is epic, and Zola will not be unworthy of it. The breadth of his undertaking, far from worrying him, will impart a new strength to him. He knows full well that once again he will have to put a great deal of himself into it, that it will not be done without difficulties, that some mornings he will sit down to work very tired and with a bitter taste in his mouth; but he knows equally well that, once he has made the initial effort his only joy will come from his work, that no other joy could come up to this one. And, by a miraculous turn of circumstances, the inspiration which he scorns and in which he hardly believes, begins to pour into his mind; the magnitude of his scope transforms his awkward prose into style. For never was a work more virile than Zola's; it seems that nothing in it is a gift from the gods, but that it is from beginning to end a hard-won victory.

His father bequeathed to him a priceless example: he never built a palace, nor a "folly," but canals, solid buildings. More an engineer than an architect, François Zola used rough materials, but he did it with indomitable courage and will. To make his canal project come true, he had to overcome a thousand difficulties, and he overcame all of them, one after the other. His son's strength is also in his courage and his obstinacy. In the work he has begun, he knows that quantity will be an intrinsic part of the quality, that it is the whole that will be judged and not a certain partial success which is for him only a detail of the architectural whole. At a single glance he saw the entire construction, just as his father saw on the drawings the canal flowing through the Aix countryside.

Zola's notations showing the hardships of the miners are brief, the same ones always reappear: the drop of water seeping from the gallery and striking the miner's face with exasperating regularity, the difficult job of pushing the coal truck in a narrow passageway. In addition to the miner's suffering, we find in *Germinal* the things that astounded the novelist during his visit. His most vivid impression was expected: the descent into darkness. The scene recurs often and, because his reaction was so strong, he paints a powerful picture of the trips in the elevator cages. He is admirable when he shows us the workers' armies running in the countryside during the strike; the roll of the wooden shoes makes the world tremble.

The barricades in *Les Misérables* resemble intellectual constructions; those who defend them are young chatterboxes who discuss philosophy before they die. In *Germinal* hatred comes from the innermost animal, injustice pushes those men and women with its painful thrust. But it is not an abstract injustice; here people do not think: the herd lunges ahead and smashes everything in its path; there is violence in these people who have suffered and seek to liberate themselves, even if it means destroying everything. Hugo shows us a revolt, Zola a revolution.

Yet, once again, Zola does not write propaganda; the novelist remains lucid; he has not yet become a prophet. In *Germinal* we do not find good people and bad, but an enormous industrial machinery exploiting man, an abstract force that crushes him. What connection could there be, as a matter of fact, between those who, in a distant city, cash in the dividends, and these miners crazed by hunger, suffering and injustice? Any human rapport is ruled out; we find ourselves in pure abstraction.

Going from the particular to the general, from the whole to the detail, Zola shows us the miner's life in all its aspects, even the most humble ones, which are not the least moving: the village fair, the love-making on the slagpiles, the minor tragedies over credit at the grocer's, the quarrels in the black houses of the compounds, the crowding of parents and children into cramped lodgings. The inventory is complete in *Germinal.*

The novelist's intuition leads Zola to anticipate one of revolution's gravest problems: the rebirth of inequality – that phoenix living in the burning heart of the revolt, ready to lunge forth into the world in his eternal shape.

Étienne, the revolutionary leader, the guiding spirit of the strike, dreams of his future, and sees himself already in parliament, speaking in the name of his class; but this single dream already isolates him from those whom he proposes to defend. He is no longer a worker who dreams; he is a leader. We feel him beginning to slide; we see the new horizons he discovers, the ambition that bites him.

This Julien Sorel of the working class does not choose the black either, but the red. Or rather he has no choice; no imperial crimson would lead him more surely to power. He feels this vaguely – still an instrument, but very nearly ready to act for himself, all the while speaking in the name of others. The distance between him and the others is already indicated, short still, but very real nonetheless; a crack through which injustice prepares to appear, to impose a new hierarchy which will replace the one that is to be abolished.

And Zola is the one whom his enemies have called a man of dangerously little knowledge! Can he have been a shortsighted psychologist, to make in passing a discovery of such importance? Of such cardinal importance that it sheds light at the heart of the most current and gravest of our problems?

On January 25, 1885, Zola gave Charpentier the good news:

> At last, my good friend, *Germinal* is finished! I am sending the last two chapters, and I ask you to write me a few words to tell me that you have received them, which will set my mind at ease. Will you please tell the printers to set up and to send me this ending immediately, because my translators are losing patience and I want to be through with the galley proofs before returning to Paris.
>
> The length of this confounded book makes me bleed for you. We will go over sixteen sheets.

> There is nothing else, except that I am happy. Ah, how I need "a little laziness!"

In spite of this victory bulletin he was not going to enjoy peace and quiet for very long. With the publication of *The Dram-shop* he had been accused of slandering the workers; the accusation comes up again about *Germinal*, with, it is true, other accusations of a totally different kind. It is about both kinds that Zola writes to Francis Magnard on April 4, 1885:

> I read M. Henry Duhamel's article this morning. He accuses me of having concocted a case of a woman working at the bottom of the mine, when he himself establishes the fact that it happened in France up to 1874, as it still happens today in Belgium. My novel takes place between 1866 and 1869. Therefore, was I not free to utilize a real fact which my drama needed? He maintains, it is true, that the novel does not bear its true date, that my strike is last year's strike at Anzin. That is a grave error; all he has to do is read: I have taken and summarized all the blood-stained strikes at the end of the Empire, around 1869, especially those at Aubin and La Ricamarie. One has but to look at the newspapers of the time. After all, since M. Duhamel agrees that two hundred women still went down in 1868, it seems to me that I had the right to have one go down in 1866.
>
> Same answer to the question of wages. We are at the end of the Empire and at a time of industrial crisis. I maintain that the wages at that time were exactly those which I have indicated. I have proofs of it in my hand, but it would be too long to list them here.
>
> But now I come to the rare accusation that I have treated the miners like a pack of drunks and libertines. M. Duhamel defends the cleanliness and the morality in the miners' tenements. All I can do is to refer to my book. I said that the houses were kept by the housewives with Flemish neatness, with some exceptions; that answers his blame of exaggerated dirtiness.
>
> As for promiscuity, and the immorality which goes with the living conditions themselves, I said that out of ten girls, six married their lovers when they became mothers; and I said also that, in households where they took in a boarder, a "lodger," one time out of two the arrangement turned into

a triangle. Such is the truth, and I hold to it. I do not wish to be contradicted on sentimental grounds; I invite people to consult statistics, to inform themselves about those places; and they will see whether I lied.

Alas! I toned the picture down. The alleviation of misery will be near at hand when people make up their minds to see the sufferings and the shame. I am accused of filthy fantasy and of premeditated mendacity about poor people who brought tears to my eyes. To each accusation I can answer with a document.

Here is the passage in *Germinal* which takes us to an auction of the coal-vein sections.

In the evening they returned together to the pit to take note of the placards. The cuttings put up to auction were in the Filonnière seam in the north gallery of the Voreux. They did not seem very advantageous, and the miner shook his head when the young man read out the conditions. On the following day when they had gone down, he took him to see the seam, and showed him how far away it was from the pit-eye, the crumbly nature of the earth, the thinness and hardness of the coal. But if they were to eat they would have to work. So on the following Sunday they went to the auction which took place in the shed and which was presided over by the engineer of the pit, assisted by the head captain, in the absence of the divisional engineer. From five to six hundred miners were there in front of the little platform which was placed in the corner, and the bidding went on so rapidly that one only heard a deep tumult of voices, of shouted figures drowned by other figures.

For a moment Maheu feared that he would not be able to obtain one of the forty workings offered by the Company. All the rivals went lower, disquieted by the rumours of a crisis and the panic of a lock-out. Négrel, the engineer, did not hurry in the face of this panic, and allowed the offers to fall to the lowest possible figures, while Dansaert, anxious to push matters still further, lied with regard to the quality of the workings. In order to get his fifty metres, Maheu struggled with a comrade who was also obstinate; in turn they each took off a centime from the tram; and if he conquered in the end it was only by lowering the wage to such an extent, that the captain, Richomme, who was standing behind him muttered between his teeth, and pushed him with the elbow, growling that he could never do it at that price.

When they came out Étienne was swearing. And he broke out before Chaval who was returning from the wheat-fields in company with Catherine, amusing himself while his father-in-law was absorbed in serious business.

"By God!" he exclaimed, "it's simply slaughter! To-day it is the worker who is forced to devour the worker!"

Chaval was furious. He would never have lowered it, he wouldn't! And Zacharie who had come out of curiosity, declared that it was disgusting. But Étienne with a violent gesture silenced them.

"It will end some day, we shall be the masters!"

Maheu, who had been mute since the auction, appeared to wake up. He repeated:

"Masters! ah! bad luck! and not too soon either."

And here is payday at the Company's yards.

The crowd of miners waits at the door of the cashier's small office; as their names are called, they enter in groups to receive their biweekly wages.

It is Maheu's turn.

"Maheu and associated, Filonnière seam, cutting No. 7. One hundred and thirty-five francs."

The cashier paid.

"Beg pardon, sir," stammered the pikeman in surprise. "Are you sure you have not made a mistake?"

He looked at this small sum of money without picking it up, frozen by a shudder which went to his heart. It was true he was expecting poor payment, but it could not come to so little or he must have calculated wrong. When he had given their shares to Zacharie, Étienne and the other mate who replaced Chaval, there would remain at most fifty francs for himself, his father, Catherine and Jeanlin.

"No, no, I've made no mistake," replied the clerk. "There were two Sundays and four rest days to be taken off; that gave you nine days of work." Maheu followed this calculation in a low voice: nine days gave him about thirty francs, eighteen to Catherine, nine to Jeanlin. As to Father Bonnemort, he only had three days. No matter, by adding the ninety francs of Zacharie and the two mates that would surely make more.

"And don't forget the fines," added the clerk. "Twenty

francs for fines for defective timbering."

The pikeman made a gesture of despair. Twenty francs of fines, four days of rest! That made out the account. To think that he had once brought back a fortnight's pay of even a hundred and fifty francs when Father Bonnemort was working and Zacharie was not yet in the household.

"Well, are you going to take it?" cried the cashier impatiently. "You can see there's someone else waiting. If you don't want it, say so."

As Maheu decided to pick up the money with his large trembling hand, the clerk stopped him.

"Wait, I have your name here. Toussaint Maheu, is it not? The general secretary wished to speak to you. Go in, he is alone."

The stunned workman found himself in an office furnished with old mahogany, upholstered with faded green rep. He listened for five minutes to the general secretary, a tall sallow gentleman, who spoke to him over the papers of his desk without rising. But the buzzing in his ears prevented him from hearing. He understood vaguely that the question of father's retirement would be taken into consideration with reference to the pension of a hundred and fifty francs, fifty years of age and forty years' service. Then it seemed to him that the secretary's voice became harder. There was a reprimand: he was accused of occupying himself with politics; an allusion was made to his lodger and the Provident Fund; finally, he was advised not to compromise himself in these follies, he, who was one of the best workmen in the mine. He wished to protest, but could only pronounce words at random, twisting his cap between his feverish fingers, and he retired, stuttering "Certainly, sir – I can assure you, sir –"

Outside, when he had found Étienne who was waiting for him, he broke out, "Well, I am a bloody fool, I ought to have replied! Not enough money to get bread, and insults as well! Yes, he has been talking against you; he told me the settlement was being poisoned. And what's to be done? Good God! Bend one's back and say thank you. He's right, that's the wisest plan."

Maheu was silent, overcome at once by rage and fear. Étienne was gloomily thinking. Once more they traversed the groups who blocked the road. The exasperation was growing, the exasperation of a calm race, the muttered warning of a storm, without violent gestures, terrible to see above this solid mass. A few who understood accounts had made calculations, and the two centimes gained by the Company over the wood were rumored about, and excited the hardest heads. But it was especially the rage over this disastrous pay, the rebellion of hunger against the rest days and the fines. Already there was not enough to eat, and what would happen if wages were still further lowered? In the *estaminets* the anger grew loud, and fury so dried their throats that the little money taken went over the counters.

From Montsou to the settlement Étienne and Maheu never exchanged a word. When the latter entered, Maheude, who was alone with the children, noticed immediately that his hands were empty.

"Well, you're a nice one!" she said. "Where's my coffee and my sugar and the meat? A bit of veal wouldn't have ruined you."

He made no reply, stifled by the emotion he had been keeping back. Then the coarse face of this man hardened to work in the mines became swollen with despair, and large tears broke from his eyes and fell in a warm rain. He had thrown himself into a chair, weeping like a child, and throwing fifty francs on the table. "Here," he stammered. "That's what I've brought you back. That's our work for all of us."

Maheude looked at Étienne, and saw that he was silent and overwhelmed. Then she also wept. How were nine people to live for a fortnight on fifty francs? Her eldest son had left them, the old man could no longer move his legs: it would soon mean death. Alzire threw herself round her mother's neck, overcome on hearing her weep. Estelle was howling, Lénore and Henri were sobbing.

And from the entire settlement there soon rose the same cry of wretchedness. The men had come back, and each household was lamenting the disaster of this bad pay. The doors opened, women appeared, crying aloud outside, as if their complaints could not be held beneath the ceilings of these small houses. A fine rain was falling, but they did not feel it; they called one another from the pavements, they showed one another in the hollow of their hands the money they had received.

"Look! They've given him this. Do they want to make fools of people?"

"As for me, see, I haven't got enough to pay the fortnight's bread with."

"And just count mine! I should have to sell my shifts!"

Maheude had come out like the others. A group had formed around the Levaque woman, who was shouting loudest of all, for her drunkard of a husband had not even turned up, and she knew that, large or small, the pay would melt away at the Volcan. Philomène watched Maheu so that Zacharie should not get hold of the money. Pierronne was the only one who seemed fairly calm, for that hypocritical Pierronne always arranged things, no one knew how, so as to have more hours on the captain's ticket than his mates. But Mother Brûlé thought this cowardly of her son-in-law; she was among the enraged, lean and erect in the midst of the group, with her fists stretched towards Montsou.

"To think," she cried, without naming the Hennebeaus, "that this morning I saw their servant go by in a carriage! Yes, the cook in a carriage with two horses, going to Marchiennes to get fish, sure enough!"

A clamour arose, and the abuse began again. That servant in a white apron taken to the market of the neighboring town in her master's carriage aroused indignation. While the workers were dying of hunger they must have their fish at all costs! Perhaps they would not always be able to eat their fish: the poor people's turn would come. The ideas sown by Étienne sprang up and expanded in this cry of revolt. It was impatience before the promised age of gold, a haste to get a share of the happiness beyond this horizon of misery, closed in like the grave. The injustice was becoming too great; at last they would demand their rights, since the bread was being taken out of their mouths. The women especially would have liked at once to take by assault this ideal city of progress, in which there was to be no more wretchedness. It was almost night; the rain increased while they were still filling the settlement with their tears in the midst of the screaming helter-skelter of the children.

That evening at the Avantage the strike was decided. Rasseneur no longer struggled against it, and Souvarine accepted it as a first step. Étienne summed up the situation in a word: if the Company really wanted a strike, then the Company should have a strike.

The strike is called; the hungry miners have been holding on for two weeks. Étienne is the source of his friends' resistance, and already ambition begins to lure him; he is intoxicated by the power of his role as leader.

Étienne was henceforth the unquestioned leader. In the evening conversations he gave forth oracles, in the degree to which study had refined him and made him able to enter into various matters. He spent the nights reading, and received a large number of letters; he even subscribed to the *Vengeur*, a Belgian socialistic paper, and this journal, the first to enter the settlement, gained for him extraordinary consideration among his mates. His growing popularity excited him more every day. To hold an extended correspondence, to discuss the fate of the workers in the four corners of the province, to give advice to the Voreux miners, especially to become a centre and to feel the world rolling round himself, was continually swelling the vanity of the former engine-man, the pikeman with greasy black hands. He was climbing a ladder, he was entering this execrated middle class, with a satisfaction to his intelligence and comfort which he did not confess to himself. He had only one trouble, the consciousness of his lack of education, which made him embarrassed and timid as soon as he was in the presence of a gentleman in a frock-coat. If he went on instructing himself, devouring everything, the lack of method would render assimilation very slow, and would produce such confusion that at last he would know much more that he could understand. So at certain hours of good sense he experienced a restlessness with regard to his mission – a fear that he was not the man for the task. Perhaps it required a lawyer, a learned man, able to speak and act without compromising the mates? But an outcry soon restored his assurance. No, no; no lawyers! They are all rascals; they profit by their knowledge to fatten on the people. Let things turn out how they will, the workers must manage their own affairs. And his dream of popular leadership again soothed him: Montsou at his feet, Paris in the misty distance, who knows? The elections some day, the tribune in a gorgeous hall, where he could thunder against the middle class in the first speech pronounced by a workman in a parliament.

But the strike order is not obeyed everyhere; in a few pits

the miners have gone back to work. During a meeting the previous day, the miners on strike have decided that they would keep their comrades from working by cutting the cables of the elevator cages, which would bring them back up from the pit.

All at once a captain passed, shouting:
"They are cutting the cables! they are cutting the cables!"
Then the panic increased. It was a furious gallop through the gloomy passages. Their heads were confused. Why cut the cables? And who was cutting them, when the men were below? It seemed monstrous.

But the voice of another captain was heard and then lost.
"The Montsou men are cutting the cables! Let everyone go up!" When he had understood, Chaval stopped Catherine short. The idea that he would meet the Montsou men up above, should he get out, paralyzed his legs. It had come, then, that band which he thought had got into the hands of the police. For a moment he thought of retracing his path and ascending through Gaston-Marie, but that was no longer possible. He swore, hesitating, hiding his fear, repeating that it was stupid to run like that. They would not, perhaps, leave them at the bottom.

The captain's voice echoed anew, now approaching them, "Let everyone go up! To the ladders! To the ladders!"

And Chaval was carried away with his mates. He pushed Catherine and accused her of not running fast enough. Did she want to remain in the pit to die of hunger? For those Montsou brigands were capable of breaking the ladders without waiting for people to come up. This abominable suggestion finished driving them wild. Along the galleries there was only a furious rush, helter-skelter; a race of madmen, each striving to arrive first and mount before the others. Some men shouted that the ladders were broken and that no one could get out. And then in frightened groups they began to reach the pit-eye, where they were all engulfed. They threw themselves toward the shaft, they crushed through the narrow door to the ladder passage; while an old groom who had prudently led the horses back to the stable, looked at them with an air of contemptuous indifference, accustomed to spend nights in the pit and certain that he could always be drawn out of it.

"By God! Will you climb in front of me?" said Chaval to

Catherine. "At least I can hold you if you fall."

Out of breath, and suffocated by this race of three kilometres which had once more bathed her in sweat, she gave herself up, without understanding, to the eddies of the crowd. Then he pulled her by the arm, almost breaking it; and she cried with pain, her tears bursting out. Already he was forgetting his oath, never would she be happy.

"Go on, then!" he roared.

But he frightened her too much. If she went first he would bully her the whole time. So she resisted, while the wild flood of their comrades pushed them to one side. The water that filtered from the shaft was falling in great drops, and the floor of the pit-eye, shaken by this tramping, was trembling over the sump, the muddy cesspool ten metres deep. At Jean-Bart, two years earlier, a terrible accident had happened just here; the breaking of a cable had precipitated the cage to the bottom of the sump, in which two men had been drowned. And they all thought of this; everyone would be left down there if they all crowded on to the planks.

"Confounded dunderhead!" shouted Chaval. "Die then; I shall be rid of you!"

He climbed up and she followed.

From the bottom of the pit to daylight there were a hundred and two ladders, about seven metres in length, each placed on a narrow landing which occupied the breadth of the passage and in which a square hole scarcely allowed the shoulders to pass. It was like a flat chimney, seven hundred metres in height, between the wall of the shaft and the brattice of the winding-cage, a damp pipe, black and endless, in which the ladders were placed one above the other, almost straight, in regular stages. It took a strong man twenty-five minutes to climb up this giant column. The passage, was no longer used except in cases of accident.

Catherine at first climbed bravely. Her naked feet were used to the hard coal on the floors of the passages, and did not suffer from the square rungs, covered with iron rods to prevent them from wearing away. Her hands, hardened by the haulage, grasped without fatigue the uprights that were too big for her. And it even interested her and took her out of her grief, this unforeseen ascent, this long serpent of men flowing on and hoisting themselves up three on a ladder, so that even when the head would emerge in daylight the tail would still be trailing over the sump. They were not there yet, the first could hardly have ascended a third of the shaft. No one spoke now, only their feet moved with a low sound; while the lamps, like travelling stars, spaced out from below upward, formed a continually increasing line.

Catherine heard a trammer behind her counting the ladders. It gave her the idea of counting them also. They had already mounted fifteen, and were arriving at a landing-place. But at that moment she fell between Chaval's legs. He swore, shouting to her to look out. Gradually the whole column stopped and became motionless. What then? Had something happened? Everyone recovered his voice to ask questions and to express his fear. Their anxiety had increased since leaving the bottom; their ignorance as to what was going on above oppressed them more as they approached daylight. Someone announced that they would have to go down again, that the ladders were broken. That was the thought that preoccupied them all, the fear of finding themselves face to face with space. Another explanation came down from mouth to mouth: there had been an accident, a pikeman slipped from a rung. No one knew exactly, the shouts made it impossible to hear; were they going to bed there? At last, without any precise information being obtained, the ascent began again, with the same slow, painful movement, in the midst of rolling feet and dancing lamps. It must certainly be higher up that the ladders were broken.

At the thirty-second ladder, as they passed a third landing-stage, Catherine felt her legs and arms grow stiff. At first she had felt a slight tingling in her skin. Now she lost the sensation of the ron and the wood beneath her feet and in her hands. A vague pain, which gradually became burning, ached in her muscles. In the dizziness which came over her, she recalled her grandfather Bonnemort's stories of the days when there was no passage; little girls often used to take out the coal on their shoulders along bare ladders; so that if one of them slipped, or a fragment of coal simply rolled out of a basket, three or four children would fall down head first from the blow. The cramp in her limbs became unbearable; she would never reach the end.

Fresh stops allowed her to breathe. But the terror which was communicated every time from above dazed her still more. Above and below her, respiration became more difficult. This interminable ascent was causing giddiness, and the nausea affected her with the others. She was suffocating, intoxicated with the darkness, exasperated with the walls which crushed against her flesh, and shuddering also with the dampness, her body perspiring beneath the great drops which fell on her. They were approaching a level where so thick a rain fell that it threatened to extinguish their lamps.

Chaval twice spoke to Catherine without obtaining any reply. What the devil was she doing down there? Had she let her tongue fall? She might just tell him if she was all right. They had been climbing for half-an-hour, but so wearily that he had only reached the fifty-ninth ladder; there were still forty-three. Catherine at last stammered that she was getting on all right. He would have treated her as a viper if she had acknowledged her weariness. The iron of the rungs must have cut her feet; it seemed to her that it was sawing in up to the bone. After every grip she expected to see her hands leave the uprights; they were so peeled and stiff that she could not close her fingers, and she feared she would fall backward with torn shoulders and disjointed thighs in this continual effort. It was especially the defective slope of the ladders from which she suffered, the almost perpendicular position which obliged her to hoist herself up by the strength of her wrists, with her belly against the wood. The panting of many breaths now drowned the sound of the feet, forming an enormous moan, multiplied tenfold by the partition of the passage, arising from the depths and expiring towards the light. There was a groan; word ran along that a trammer had just cut open his head at the edge of a stair.

And Catherine went on climbing. They had passed the level. The rain had ceased; a mist made heavy the cellar-like air, poisoned with the odour of old iron and damp wood. Mechanically she continued to count in a low voice – eighty-one, eighty-two, eighty-three; still nineteen. The repetition of these figures supported her merely by their rythmic balance; she had no further consciousness of her movements. When she lifted her eyes the lamps turned in a spiral. Her blood was flowing; she felt that she was dying; the least breath would have knocked her over. The worst was that those below were now pushing, and that the entire column was rushing on, yielding to the growing anger of its fatigue, the furious need to see the sun again. The first mates had emerged; there were, then, no broken ladders; but the idea that they might yet be broken to prevent the last from coming up, when others were already breathing up above, nearly drove them mad. And when a new stoppage occurred oaths broke out, and all went on climbing, hustling each other, passing over each other's bodies to arrive at all costs.

Then Catherine fell. She had cried Chaval's name in despairing appeal. He did not hear; he was struggling, digging his heels into a comrade's ribs to get before him. And she was rolled down and trampled over. As she fainted she dreamed. It seemed to her that she was one of the little putter-girls of old days, and that a fragment of coal, fallen from the basket above her, had thrown her to the bottom of the shaft, like a sparrow struck by a flint. Five ladders only remained to climb. It had taken nearly an hour. She never knew how she reached daylight, carried up by the shoulders, supported by the throttling narrowness of the passage. Suddenly she found herself in the dazzling sunlight, in the midst of a yelling crowd which was hooting her.

Germinal made an enormous impression; it revealed a universe which those whom it worried would have preferred to ignore. The work was so powerful that it established Zola as one of the greatest writers of all time. After *The Dram-shop*, *Nana*, and *Germinal*, no one could doubt that their author had extraordinary stamina.

He also claimed a certain philosophy. To Gustave Geoffroy, who had published an essay on *Germinal*, Émile Zola addressed the following profession of faith on July 22, 1885:

> You are right; I believe that in my works people must look above all for a particular philosophy of life. My role has been to put man back in his place within the world, like a product of the earth still subject to all the influences of the milieu; and, in man himself, I have put the brain back in its proper place among the organs, for I do not believe that thought is anything other than a function of matter. The field of psychology, so talked about today, is no more than an abstraction, and in any case it would only be a small part of physiology.

DEMANDEZ *GERMINAL!* LE NOUVEAU JOUET DE L'ANNÉE!

Illustration by Gil Baër
(*La Chronique parisienne*, Dec. 27, 1885)

Caricature by Jean Veber (1887)

The End of the Rougon-Macquart

A year later, in 1886, *The Masterpiece* (*L'Oeuvre*) appeared; it put a definite end to the friendship between Cézanne and Zola. The painter recognized himself in the portrait, and the discord between the two men came out in the open.

In June of that same year, Zola explains to J. van Santen Kolff what he intends to accomplish by writing *Earth (La Terre)*:

... I am still working on the plan of my next novel, *Earth*; I shall begin to write in about two weeks. This novel frightens even me for, in its simplicity, it will be one of the fullest. I want to put in it all our farm people with all their history, their customs, their role in our life; I want to pose the sociological question of property; I wish to show where we are going in this agricultural crisis, so grave at this point. Every time I begin to study something, I run into socialism. I should like to do for the peasant in *Earth* what I did for the worker in *Germinal*.... Add to that the fact that I wish to remain an artist and a writer, to write the living poem of the earth: the seasons, the work in the field, the people, the animals, all of country life.... And that is all I can tell you, because otherwise I would have to go into explanations which I do not have the courage for. You might say that mine is

Paris 13 octobre 87

Mon cher Goncourt,

Hier soir seulement, des amis communs m'ont appris une très étonnante chose : vous m'accuseriez d'avoir fait dire que vous étiez l'inspirateur volontaire de l'article imbécile et ordurier publié par "le Figaro". Vous me croyez donc bête ? Faites-moi l'amitié de penser que je sais comment l'article a été écrit. Je suis convaincu, j'ai répété partout que, si vous en aviez eu connaissance, vous en auriez empêché la publica-

the huge ambition to put the whole life of the peasant in my book: the work, the loves, the politics, the religion, the past, the present, the future; and you will know the truth. But have I the strength to tackle such a large order? Well, anyway, I shall attempt it....

This book, published the following year, will bring about one of the most violent storms which Zola had to face. It was said that he slandered the farmers, and that his indecency went too far this time. The adversaries of naturalism were shooting at close range. One bit of help they had not counted on came to them from a group of young writers who published a manifesto repudiating Zola as their master. These five so-called disciples were J. H. Rosny, Lucien Descaves, Paul Bonnetain, Paul Marguerite, and Gustave Guiches. Zola's surprise was great, for he knew them very slightly.

On August 19, 1887, he will write to Henry Bauer:

> Your letter touched me, my dear Bauer, and as you say, if the odious side of the article in question hurt me for a while, the good greetings that come to me have already consoled me.
>
> You allude to some shady details which I obstinately refuse to notice. Fortunately none of the five signers is a friend of mine, not one has been in my house, I have never seen them except at Goncourt's or Daudet's. This made their manifesto less difficult for me to take. I have always been afflicted by solitude and unpopularity; I have only a few friends, and I value them highly.

Zola is right not to consider Goncourt or Daudet, as suggested to him, the instigators of the manifesto. Indeed they have nothing to do with it. Daudet wrote Zola to beware of those who would pit them against each other.

To that he answers on November 19, 1887:

> I have never thought, my dear Daudet, that you had known about the five's manifesto! My first reaction was that neither you nor Goncourt knew anything of it, and that the article must have shocked you considerably. That is what I said to the reporters, without any ulterior motive and with the firmest conviction. I am dumbfounded that you have taken it as an indirect accusation on my part. What baffles me is that from the victim you made me the culprit, and that instead of sending me a friendly greeting, you almost broke

up with me. You must admit that this was going a little too far.

I have never been angry with you. I know very well how the manifesto was written, and it makes me smile. Your letter, my dear Daudet, does in spite of all make me quite happy, since it puts an end to a misunderstanding which had already enchanted our enemies.

It is in 1888 that Zola meets Jeanne Rozerot. She is a young woman of twenty, and he is forty-eight. The author has never had any children; Jeanne will give him two, a boy and a girl, whom Madame Zola will acknowledge after her husband's death. This will be Zola's only love affair.

The same year, wishing once more to show that he can go from the violent to the delicate, Émile Zola published *The Dream* (*Le Rêve*). But he comes back two years later to his true inspiration with *The Human Beast* (*La Bête Humaine*), which is in the pure naturalistic tradition.

As early as 1889, he was gathering the material; on June 3, he wrote Doctor Gouverné:

> I need an item of information for the novel I am writing, and I take the liberty of asking you for it.
>
> I understand that saltpeter is a hypnotizing poison. Could a person be poisoned by the saltpeter found in our houses? I want a rascally peasant to poison his wife in a slow and easy way.
>
> Can I have him give her the saltpeter at his disposal, and in what quantity, and how often?

And for the first time, it appears in a letter to Charpentier that he is somewhat impatient to finish his series.

> I have worked furiously at my novel. I shall certainly finish by the first of December.
>
> I feel a strong desire to finish the *Rougon-Macquart* series as soon as possible. I should like to be rid of it by January, 1892. It is possible, but I shall have to buckle down hard.
>
> I am going through a very healthy period of work, I am feeling admirably well, and I find myself the way I was at twenty, when I wanted to eat mountains.
>
> Ah, my friend, if only I were thirty again, you would see what I could do. I would astonish the world.

The Human Beast is nothing but a series of murders. The

LE RÊVE

DRAME LYRIQUE EN QUATRE ACTES, D'APRÈS LE ROMAN D'ÉMILE ZOLA

Première représentation le 18 juin 1891

Poème de Louis GALLET — **Musique de Alfred BRUNEAU**

ACTE II. — SCÈNE III. — **Au son des Cloches**

Publié avec l'autorisation spéciale de MM. Choudens fils, éditeurs-propriétaires de la partition *Le Rêve*.

principal character, Jacques Lantier, is a born criminal, by heredity of course. Just as others have a passion for alcohol, he has a taste for blood. While other characters in *The Human Beast* become assassins out of interest or jealousy, Lantier is one instinctively, gratuitously, for the pure and simple joy of killing. And his struggle against his desire to kill is admirably described.

Nothing could better demonstrate the difference between Dostoevsky and Zola than a comparison between *Crime and Punishment* and *The Human Beast*. Raskolnikov kills for metaphysical reasons, his tragedy is one of sin, and redemption at any cost, even punishment. In *The Human Beast* animality alone is master. Everything happens inside the body; obscure laws rule men, and thought means nothing. The result of the crime is not torment of the soul, a drama of the conscience, but a slow and implacable decomposition of the criminal.

Zola is perhaps never any greater than when he shows the dwindling of all strength and energy in man. This writer, so strict with himself, this eager worker, achieves the maximum of his genius when he describes the inner collapse, the rotting of one of his characters. Only then does he attain a genuine profundity.

The Human Beast takes up the theme of *Thérèse Raquin* again, but what was only a straight tale has broadened. Taken up again by the mature writer, the original novel by the young Zola grows richer with the power of the master.

In this one as in the other, a man and a woman kill, and what we see are the consequences of the crime. But the backdrop is admirable: the locomotives, the railroad stations, and that then new sensation of speed are used like a gigantic set in chapter after chapter with spellbinding force. *The Human Beast* is the story of a crime of passion in an industrial universe.

People smiled about the trip that Zola took on the platform of a locomotive from Paris to Nantes, dressed in an engineer's blue suit. Edmond de Goncourt, snug in his Japanese living room, was to gloat over it. It is easy to see, however, how such an interest in learning firsthand – down to the most minute details – about what he writes, adds truth and life to his novel. Here is the passage where Jacques Lantier, predisposed by heredity to becoming an assassin, and who knows it and fears it every minute, learns that his mistress Séverine has participated in a crime:

In Séverine, after the mounting heat of this long recital, this cry was like the very flowering of her need of happiness, her execration of her memories. But Jacques, burning like her, still held her back.

"No, no, wait.... So you flattened yourself on his legs, and you felt him die?" In him, the unknown was awakening; a savage flood rose from his guts, filled his skull, made his eyes see red. He was the prey again of his curiosity in murder. "And so, the knife, you felt it penetrate?"

"Yes, a dull blow."

"Ah! A dull blow.... Not a ripping, you're sure?"

"No, no, just a shock."

"And then, he had a shudder, eh?"

"Yes, three shudders, oh! From one end of his body to the other, so long I felt them go right down to his feet."

"Shudders that stiffened him, eh?"

"Yes, the first very strong, the other two weaker."

"And he died, and what did it do to you, to feel him die like that, by a knife?"

"To me? Oh, I don't know."

"You don't know? Why do you lie? Tell me! Tell me what it did to you, frankly. Did it make you suffer?"

"No, no, no suffering!"

"Pleasure?"

"Pleasure! Ah, no, not pleasure!"

"What then, my love? Please, tell me everything.... If you knew.... Tell me what one feels."

"My God, can such things be said in words? It's frightful, it carries you away, oh, so far, so far! I lived more in that minute than in all my life before."

Teeth clenched, stammering only now, Jacques had taken her this time. And Séverine was also taking him. They possessed each other, finding love again in the depths of death, in the same painful voluptuousness of beasts who gut themselves in their rut. The only sound was that of their hoarse breathing. The bloody reflection had disappeared from the ceiling; and, the fire out, the room was beginning to freeze with the terrific cold from out-of-doors. Not a voice rose from Paris muffled in snow. For a moment, there were snores from the apartment of the newsvendor next door. Then everything had fallen into the black gulf of silence in the sleeping house.

Jacques, who had held Séverine in his arms, felt her yielding at once to invincible slumber. The journey, the long wait in Misard's house, this feverish night, had exhausted her. She muttered a childish good night, and was already asleep, breathing evenly. The cuckoo-clock had just sung out that it was three o'clock.

For nearly an hour longer, Jacques held her with his left arm, which slowly grew numb. He could not close his eyes; an obstinate, invisible hand seemed to open them in the darkness. Now he could see nothing in the room, where everything had disappeared in darkness, the stove, the furniture, the walls. And he had to turn to make out the two pale squares of the windows, motionless in the dark, lightly pale as in a dream. In spite of his crushing fatigue, a prodigious cerebral activity kept him alert, going over and over the same thoughts. Every time that, by an effort of will, he seemed about to slip off to sleep, the same haunting visions passed before him, awakening the same sensations. The scenes that unrolled before him, with mechanical regularity, while his staring eyes darkened, were those of the murder, detail after detail. Always they recurred, identical, overpowering, maddening. The knife cut into the throat with a dull shock, the body shuddered three times, and the life flowed in a gush of warm blood, a red flood he seemed to feel run over his hands. Twenty, thirty times the knife penetrated, the body shuddered. It was growing, stifling him, bursting the night. Oh! To give such a knife thrust himself, to satisfy the fountain of his distant longing, know what one feels, taste of that minute wherein one lives more than in all one's life before!

His excitement increased, and Jacques thought perhaps Séverine's weight on his arm kept him from sleeping. He freed himself gently, without waking her. At first he was relieved, and breathed more freely, thinking that sleep was coming at last. But in spite of his efforts, invisible fingers kept opening his eyes again, and in the darkness the murder scene appeared before him in red, the knife struck, the body shuddered. A bloody mist filled the darkness, the wound in the throat, growing larger, yawned like a cut made with an ax. Then he struggled no longer, but lay on his back and stared at the persistent vision. He could hear the working of his brain inside his skull, like a machine rumbling and roaring. It came from far back, from his youth. He had thought he was cured, for this passion had died months ago with the possession of this woman. But he had never felt it so intensely as now, under the influence of the murder about which, a while ago, she had whispered while pressed against his body, bound to his members. He had drawn aside, avoiding her touch, burning at the slightest touch of her skin. An insupportable wave of heat crept up his spine, as though the mattress under him had changed to live coals. He felt a prickling, like red-hot needles, on the back of his neck. He tried putting his hands outside the covers, but they immediately turned icy, and he shivered. He grew frightened of his hands, and at first clasped them on his stomach, then slipped them under his buttocks, holding them tightly down, imprisoning them, as though he feared they would commit some abomination, an act he did not desire, but would nevertheless commit.

He counted the strokes each time the cuckoo sang. Four o'clock, five o'clock, six o'clock. He waited for the dawn, hoping it would drive away the nightmare. He turned toward the windows and stared at them, but there was no light but the vague reflection of the snow. At a quarter to five, he had heard the express come in from Le Havre, only forty minutes late, which showed that communication was reestablished. It was not until after seven o'clock he saw the panes whiten, turn milky pale very slowly. Finally, the room grew light, with that confused glimmer in which the furniture seems to float. The stove reappeared, the closet, the sideboard. He could not close his eyelids, but his eyes grew irritated, wanting to see. All at once, even before it grew light enough, he guessed at, rather than saw, on the table, the knife he had used the night before to cut the cake. He saw nothing but this little pointed knife. The increasing daylight that now streamed in through the two windows was all reflected on that narrow blade. His terror of his hands made him plunge them deeper beneath his body, for he felt them growing restless, rebellious, stronger than his will. Had they ceased to belong to him? Hands that came to him from another, hands inherited from an ancestor of the time when men strangled the beasts in the forest.

Jacques turned toward Séverine, to stop looking at the knife. She slept peacefully, breathing like a tired child. Her heavy black hair, unknotted, darkened her pillow, flowing down to her shoulders; between the curls, under her chin, he could see her throat, milky, delicate, scarcely pink. He looked at her as though he did not know her at all. And yet he adored her, carried her image everywhere with him, desiring her so that his yearning sometimes tortured him even while he drove his locomotive, to such an extent that one day he had awakened just as he passed full speed through a station, against the signals. But the sight of that white throat completely, inexorably, fascinated him; and within him, with still conscious horror, he felt an imperious and growing urge to go to the table, take that knife, and plunge it to the handle in that woman's flesh. He heard the dull shock of the blade entering, saw the body shudder and twitch three times, then stiffen in death, in a red flood. Struggling to tear himself free of this vision, he lost more of his will every moment, as though overpowered by a fixed idea which, when it conquered him, would make him yield to his instinctive impulse. Everything grew confused. His rebellious hands escaped from their confinement. He understood so well that he was no longer their master, and that they would take brutal satisfaction if he continued to look at Séverine, that he spent his last effort of will throwing himself out of the bed, rolling on the floor like a drunken man. He picked himself up, and almost fell again as he tripped over the skirts that lay about. He swayed about, seeking his clothes with a wondering hand, thinking only of dressing quickly, taking the knife and going down to the street to kill another woman. This time, his desire tortured him too much; he had to kill. He could not find his pants, and laid his hand on them three times before he realized it. It was painful to have to put on his shoes. Though it was broad daylight now, the room seemed to him to be full of red smoke on an icy, foggy dawn, with all precision lost. He shivered in a fever. He was fully dressed now, and he picked up the knife, hid it in his sleeve, certain he would kill the first woman he met on the sidewalk. A rustle of linen and a prolonged sigh from the bed froze him to the spot, standing by the table. He turned pale.

It was Séverine awakening.

"Why, dear, are you going out already?"

He did not answer, nor look at her, hoping she would drop

back to sleep.

"Where are you going, dear?"

"Nothing," he said, "something to do with my work. Go to sleep, I'll be back."

She answered sleepily, sinking back into a torpor, her eyes already closed again.

"Oh, I'm so sleepy, so sleepy.... Come and kiss me, dear."

But he did not move, for he knew that if he turned around, with that knife in his hand, if he only saw her, so delicate and pretty in her disordered nakedness, it was the end of all control over himself. In spite of himself, his hand would lift, and plunge the knife into her throat.

"Darling, come and kiss me...."

Her voice died out, and she fell gently to sleep again, with a caressing murmur. He opened the door and fled.

On March 9, 1890, writing to Jules Lemaître, Zola admits again that he is beginning to grow tired of *The Rougon-Macquart*: "To be sure I am growing tired of my series, between you and me. But I do have to finish it nonetheless, without changing my methods too much."

In 1870, he was almost made a prefect; now he is offered the position of deputy in parliament. In the name of a group of young people, Clément Janin offers him a candidacy in the fifth ward of Paris. Zola answers him:

> I am terribly touched and flattered by your offer. But I have absolutely too much work to do, my literary enterprises forbid me to accept it. The mandate of a deputy is one of the heaviest I know of, when one does not wish to be an idle deputy; and since I am a man of conscience and labor, I prefer to finish my work.

This work on the other hand will go on growing weaker. The three novels published between 1891 and 1893, *Money (L'Argent), The Downfall (La Débâcle), Doctor Pascal (Le Docteur Pascal)*, which mark the end of *The Rougon-Macquart*, no longer have the same vigor. But books have singular destinies. *The Downfall*, one of the least successfully written, has one of the largest printings. The concern for current reality did not help the writer on an artistic level, but it contributed to the book's commercial success.

In answer to J. van Santen Kolff who asked him about the composition of *The Downfall*, Zola writes:

I followed my usual method; walks around the places that I shall have to describe; reading all the written documents which are extraordinarily numerous; finally long conversations with those authors of the tragedy whom I could meet. Here is what helped me most for *The Downfall*. When the war was declared there were, among the liberal professions, the lawyers, the young professors, even the university teachers, and the old professors without a position, people of high learning, not drafted, but exempted in fact, who enlisted voluntarily as privates. In the evening, around the bivouac, they jotted down their impressions, their adventures in little notebooks. Five or six of them were offered to me, sometimes the original, sometimes a copy; one or two of them were even printed. What was especially interesting to me was the life, the lived moment. They all resembled one another. There was uniformity of impressions. All that, the very basis of *The Downfall,* was given to me in those notebooks.

However, the little note cards with the names of the regiments, the field charts, noting the advances and the setbacks of the armies, the names of the generals, and even those soldiers' diaries that he read, do not help him succeed in giving an impression of life. If we compare *The Downfall* to *War and Peace* we can see what Tolstoy achieved with a similar subject.

In *Doctor Pascal,* Zola painted himself in the most flattering light; the "master" is good-looking, generous, intelligent, childishly unselfish. Never had Zola been so taken by one of his characters. Dishwater and perspiration marks are replaced by lilies and roses; desires are so sublimated that, when the "master" becomes the lover of a girl twenty-five years younger than he, it is as if an archangel were gently bending over a saint.

Who said that Zola saw humanity under a gray sky? What has become of the experimental novel, of its scientific rigor? The leader of the naturalistic school has a decided gift for the sententious. This will be only too obvious in the rest of his works, when the sermon appears.

Up till now he had had the wisdom of drawing the line between criticism and the novel. He did maintain that the latter came out of the former, but – happily carried away in his best books – he showed us groups endowed with a life of their own,

Caricature by Gilbert Martin (1890)

characters marvelously alive. In what he will call the constructive part of his work, the author will be omnipresent, all the ideas expressed will be his. The prophet will replace the novelist. The fault for which he so heatedly blamed Hugo will become his.

When Zola finishes his series, he is fifty-three years old; he had begun it in 1871, at thirty-one. In the space of twenty-two years then, he has written twenty novels consisting of thirty-one volumes and peopled by twelve hundred characters. On the shelves of his Médan library, Zola can contemplate that row of books to which are added translations in most of the European languages.

He would have the right to rest but he does not consider it. New works, for which he makes plans, begin to haunt him. Already he has the general title: *The Three Cities* which will be *Lourdes, Rome, Paris*. He still confronts the challenge of Balzac's *Human Comedy*, trying to equal in strength the man whom he admires the most. But he will work in a completely different frame of mind from now on. The naturalistic novelist has been accused so often of showing nothing but the weaknesses of society that Zola wants to prove now the ill-founded character of that criticism. It is with this new purpose in mind that he again sets to work.

à ma chère femme
à ma bien-aimée Jeanne

Emile Zola

LOURDES

2e DIVISION	RÉPUBLIQUE FRANÇAISE	AUTORISATION
3e BUREAU	PRÉFECTURE DE POLICE	N° 51038
2e SECTION		

M. *Zola, Emile*
demeurant *21 bis Rue de Bruxelles*
est autorisé à circuler en vélocipède dans les rues de Paris, à charge par lui de se conformer aux prescriptions de l'ordonnance de police du 9 novembre 1874, dont extrait est ci-contre.

Paris, le *19 8bre* 1895

POUR LE PRÉFET DE POLICE :
Le Secrétaire général,

Signature du Titulaire,

Emile Zola

Imp. CHAIX (Succ. B), rue de la Sainte-Chapelle, 5. — 1627-95

Next page: about the same time, on foot, and in front of a backdrop

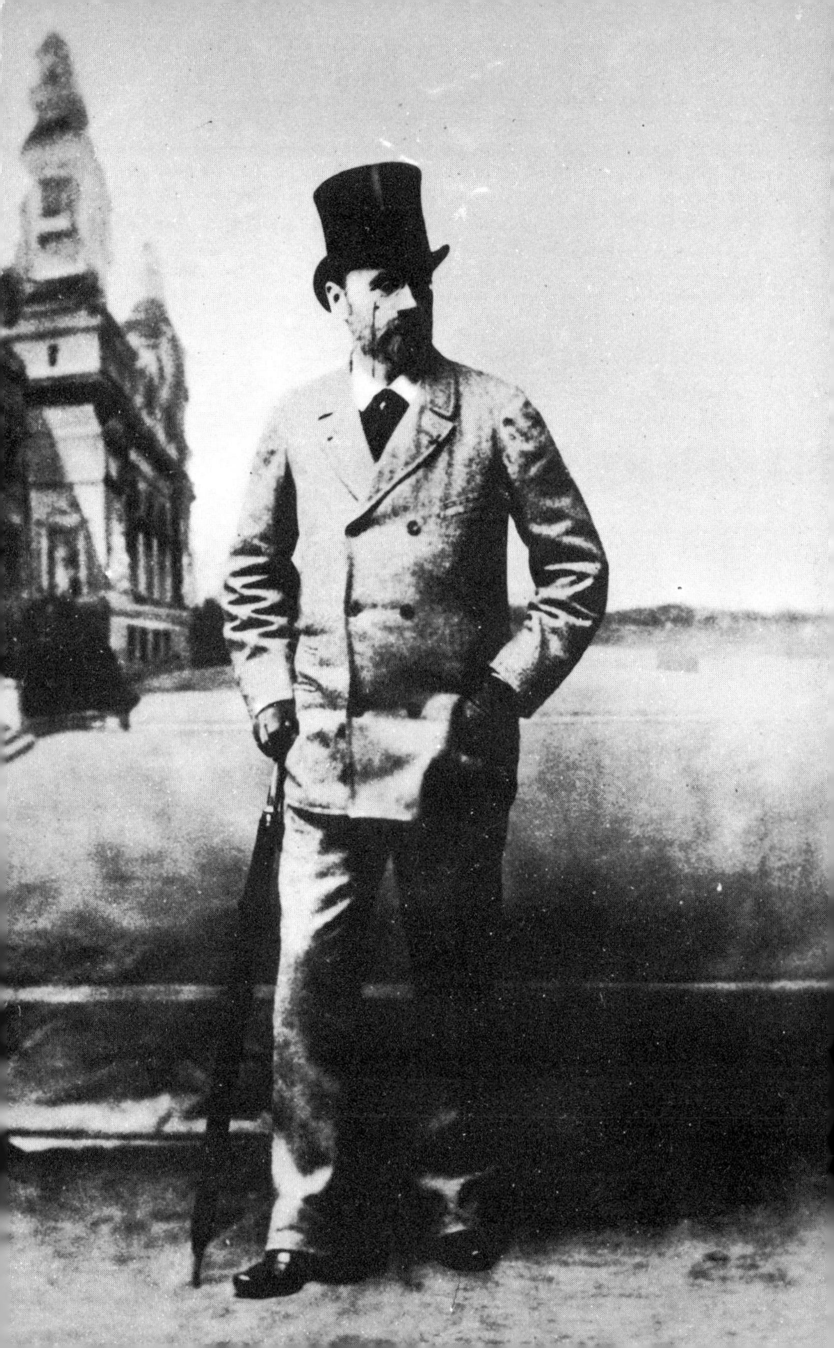

Drawing by Steinlen (September 1897)

The Dreyfus Case

Rome and *Paris* will appear in 1896 and 1897.

In 1894 Zola is in Italy where he is gathering information for the first of those two books. Then he comes back to Médan and continues to work. On October 15, 1894, Captain Dreyfus is arrested; on December 22, he is sentenced to life imprisonment on Devil's Island.

In 1894, at the time the Dreyfus affair began, I was in Rome, and I did not come back until around the 15th of December. There, of course, I did not read the French newspapers very much. That explains my ignorance, the kind of indifference in which I remained for a long time about the case. It was not until November 1897, when I came back from the country, that I began to get interested; certain circumstances had allowed me to find out some facts and see certain documents published later which made my convictions absolutely unshakable.

In the beginning no one doubts Dreyfus' guilt; even those who will become his most ardent supporters, Clémenceau and Jaurès, attack him violently. Slowly the rumor gets around Paris that the captain might be innocent. In 1896 an officer,

Lieutenant-Colonel Picquart, informs his superiors of his conviction that Esterhazy is the real culprit, the author of the memorandum sent to Germany. But he is kept quiet and sent on a mission to North Africa. The offices of the Ministry of War do not care to re-open a closed incident. They think that the army's prestige would suffer from a revision of the trial because it would show how arbitrarily the case was conducted.

If Zola lived in Paris, no doubt he would listen to the rumors, whispered from ear to ear, that are beginning to circulate in the city. But he is living in Médan, completely taken up by his trilogy; he is ignorant of the Dreyfus affair, or at least he does not give it more attention than is warranted by a routine case of treason.

However the unrest grows. The vice-president of the Senate, Scheurer-Kestner, a man of irreproachable integrity, unanimously respected, is feeling doubtful himself. It is less easy to keep him quiet than a career officer. He throws his moral weight into the struggle that now begins. Moreover Dreyfus' letters to his family are beginning to be known; they have a moving tone. Guarded night and day by twelve men in his island prison, the prisoner claims his innocence with such consistency and bitterness that some consciences begin to get disturbed. Finally Bernard Lazare gets into the fray, openly alerting public opinion. From then on, as Zola will write later, *Truth is on the march, nothing will stop it.*

Still the writer is not yet caught by that fever of justice which will slowly set France afire.

It is only around the end of 1897, arriving to spend the winter in his Paris apartment, that he gets acquainted with certain documents, and that the facts appear to him in all their clarity. For the first time in the more than thirty years that he has been writing, he sees a reason for action which takes precedence over his urge to create; it is a matter of denouncing a crime perpetrated in the face of a whole people.

Zola's moments of hesitation are always short. At the same moment when he understands the justice and necessity of an act, he ushers it into the realm of reality. For him there is no distance between thought and action, and this sometimes makes him seem naïve as certain pages of *The Experimental Novel* do. But this time he treads on solid ground; it is no longer a matter of intellectual speculation, but of an injustice to redress.

How will his protest take shape, where will it express itself?

While he feels he is ready for the fight, he still lacks a plan of attack. He knows that the struggle will be arduous; he knows already how those who have doubted the equity of the judgment have been treated, but it cannot stop him. His courage is unflinching, thirty years of literary polemic have steeled it. He will not join the clan of those who whisper their doubts, who murmur the truth. Barrès will say that he had a tinge of opportunism. He did indeed have the sense to see an opportunity to take the side of justice, bravely and unafraid of the blows. At such a time as our own, when Dreyfus affairs threaten to become daily occurrences, Zola's example holds up well.

Chance will decide the way in which the author will go into action. During a walk through Paris, Zola meets Fernand de Rodays, the editor of *Figaro*. It is December, 1897; what would the two of them talk about other than what has become "The Affair?" De Rodays shares Zola's conviction: Dreyfus is innocent. A few days later in his newspaper Zola's first article appears entitled, *For the Record (Procès-Verbal)* – (December 5, 1897). The author condemns, among other things, anti-Semitism. The "hazy brain" to which he alludes is of course Édouard Drumont, the author of *Jewish France (La France Juive)*.

And now, anti-Semitism.

There is the culprit. I have already noted how this barbaric campaign which throws us back a thousand years, arouses my need for fraternity, my passion for tolerance and human emancipation. To go back to the religious wars, to resort again to persecutions, to wish for races to exterminate one another, is so meaningless in our century of liberation, that such a proposition seems above all stupid. It could only have been born in the hazy, ill-balanced brain of a fanatic, of the great vanity of a writer long unknown, wishing at all cost to play a part, even an odious one. And I cannot think that such a movement will have a decisive importance in France, this country of free-will, of brotherly generosity and clear sightedness.

Yet terrible harm has already been done, I must confess. The poison is in the people, if the people are not already completely poisoned. We can thank anti-Semitism for the dangerous virulence which the Panama scandals have taken on in our country. And this deplorable Dreyfus affair is its work: it alone frightens the crowds, and keeps this error from being quietly, nobly recognized for the sake of our health and our good name. Is there anything simpler, more natural than to tell the truth when doubts become serious, and is it so improbable that there must be a hidden poison in us, which makes us all delirious, otherwise would we take part in such madness?

That poison is the enraged hatred of the Jews, fed to the people every morning for years. There is a band of professional poisoners, and the worst of it is that they do it in the name of morality, in the name of Christ, as avengers and judges. And who says that the atmosphere in which the court martial sat did not influence its decisions? A Jewish traitor selling his country, that goes over without debate. If no human reason can explain the crime – if he is rich, wise, hard-working, steady, lives an impeccable life – is it not enough that he is a Jew?

Today, since we have been asking for some light, the attitude of anti-Semitism is more violent, more repulsive than ever. If the proofs are investigated, and if a Jew's innocence were proven, what a blow for the anti-Semites! How could there be an innocent Jew? A whole arrangement of lies would topple; there would be light, good faith, justice – the very ruin of a sect that influences crowds of simple people by means of insults and impudent slander.

That is once again what we have witnessed: the furor of these public enemies when they thought that a little light was to be shed. And we have seen also, alas, the confusion of the crowd which they have contaminated, the whole of public opinion bewildered. The dear and humble people who persecute the Jews today, would tomorrow start a revolution to free Captain Dreyfus, if only some honest man instilled in them the sacred fire of justice.

On December 14, his *Letter to the Youth* is sold in the form of a pamphlet.

Young people, remember the sufferings your fathers have endured, the terrible battles they had to fight in order to win the freedom which you now enjoy. If you feel independent, if you may come and go freely, say what you think in the newspapers, have an opinion and express it publicly, it is because your fathers gave of their intelligence and of their blood. You were not born in tyranny; you do not know what it is to wake up each morning with the master's boot on your chest; you have not fought to escape the sword of the dictator or the false values of a bad judge. Thank your fathers, and do not commit the crime of acclaiming lies, of fighting side by side with brutal force, fanatic intolerance and voracious ambition. If you do, dictatorship awaits you in the end.

Young people, always get on the side of justice. If your idea of justice were to become confused, you would be headed for all kinds of danger. And I am not speaking of the justice of our Codes, which is nothing more than the guarantee of our social ties. To be sure we must respect them, but there is a higher ideal of justice, that which proposes that any judgment of man is fallible, and admits the innocence of a condemned man without having to feel that it insults the judges. Is that not an adventure that should arouse your passion for justice? Who will rise to demand that justice be done, if it is not you who are not in our selfish grown-up struggles, you who are not yet engaged nor compromised in any shady affairs, you who can speak loud and clear and in good faith?

Young people! Be humane, be generous. Even if we make a mistake, be on our side when we say that an innocent man is being subjected to dreadful suffering, and that our rebelling heart is broken with anguish. If we admit for a single moment the possible error, in the light of such exaggerated punishment, our chest tightens, tears come to our eyes. Of course, the guards remain insensitive, but how can you? You who are still weeping, you who must be broken to all kinds of misery and pity! Why is it you do not have that chivalrous dream of defending the cause of any martyr felled by hatred, and of liberating him? Who will, if you do not, attempt the sublime adventure, plunge headlong into a dangerous and superb cause, take a stand against the people, in the name of justice? And finally are you not ashamed that the elders, the old ones, are the ones who are reacting passionately, who are doing your job of generous impulse?

The intervention of this new fighter spreads dismay among the adversaries: he brings his stature, his taste for fighting, his talent for controversy, the authority given him by his works, which in France alone run into hundreds of thousands of copies. Immediately, people like Léon Bloy, Barbey d'Aurevilly, Rochefort, Ernest Judet, Drumont, Barrès, Maurras concentrate their attacks on Zola: any weapon goes, even the most odious, and in a *Petit Journal* article, Judet will go as far as to question the integrity of his father, François Zola.

At the time the author gets into the fray, the anti-Dreyfus sentiment is extraordinarily violent. With very few exceptions, people of the Left remain quite silent. The dividing line is determined less by political affiliations than by each man's scruples. The Affair remains a question of conscience.

The Dreyfus case was judged in a real atmosphere of progrom.

A "Catholic bank" – founded to put a check on Protestant and Jewish bankers – having failed a little before the Affair, its work immediately degenerated into a racial and social one. Drumont had prepared the terrain with his pamphlet. *Le Petit Journal*, with a circulation of one million, was spreading lies and hatred into the most remote villages. Consequently, many people, although they were convinced of Dreyfus' innocence, abstained from taking a stand publicly.

Zola publishes his various articles nonetheless. His famous letter to Félix Faure, known by the title of "*I accuse*" ("*J'accuse*"), which Clémenceau gave to it, appears in *L'Aurore*. With admirable foresight and courage, he denounces the machinations that surrounded the trial; this letter causes him to be sent to jail for a year and to be fined three thousand francs.

Zola then goes to England where he stays eleven months, assuming the role of a conspirator, calling himself "Pascal," receiving coded telegrams from France, and beginning to write the first volume of his *Four Gospels: Fecundity*.

When he hears that the sentence will be re-examined, he returns; but the military machine wins again: Dreyfus is pronounced guilty a second time by the court martial. Zola's indignation bursts out in a new article.

It is, however, the last victory for the Ministry of War; from now on the truth will rise on all sides. Colonel Henry commits suicide, Colonel Esterhazy flees abroad, Dreyfus is freed.

Freed, but not yet reinstated. He will have to wait until 1906. However, the moral victory is complete although there is still an air of clemency where there should be complete reparation of an injustice. In his letter to Mme. Alfred Dreyfus,

L'AURORE

Littéraire, Artistique, Sociale

J'Accuse…!

LETTRE AU PRÉSIDENT DE LA RÉPUBLIQUE

Par ÉMILE ZOLA

Conspuez Zola!

Taken from "Ulk" (Berlin, February 4, 1898)

Colonel Henry's suicide

RÈGLE
de
L'AFFAIRE DREYFUS
et de la
VÉRITÉ

U JEU

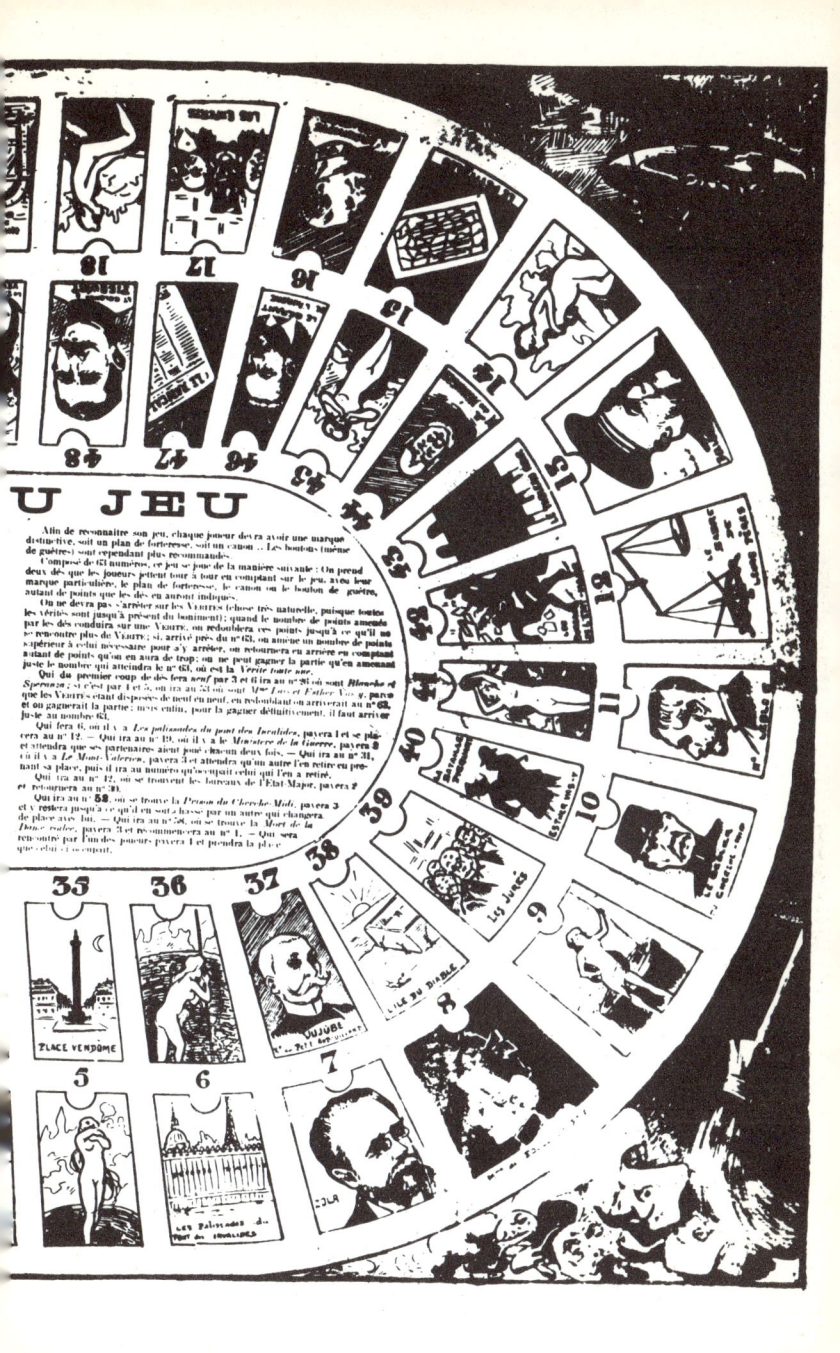

Afin de reconnaître son jeu, chaque joueur devra avoir une marque distinctive, soit un plan de forteresse, soit un canon.. Les boutons même de guêtres sont cependant plus recommandés.

Composé de 63 numéros, ce jeu se joue de la manière suivante : On prend deux dés que les joueurs jettent tour à tour en comptant sur le jeu, avec leur marque particulière, le plan de forteresse, le canon ou le bouton de guêtre, autant de points que les dés en auront indiqués.

On ne devra pas s'arrêter sur les Vxxrrs (chose très naturelle, puisque toutes les vérités sont jusqu'à présent du boniment); quand le nombre de points amené par les dés conduira sur une Vxxrry, on redoublera ces points jusqu'à ce qu'il ne se rencontre plus de Vxxrrv; si, arrivé près du n° 63, on amène un nombre de points supérieur à celui nécessaire pour s'y arrêter, on retournera en arrière en comptant autant de points qu'on en aura de trop; on ne peut gagner la partie qu'en amenant juste le nombre qui atteindra le n° 63, où est la *Vérité toute nue*.

Qui, du premier coup de dés fera *neuf* par 3 et 6 ira au n° 31 où sont *Blanche et Sprana* etc., c'est par 4 et 5, ou ira au 33 où sont M.me Luc et Esther Vx., y, parce que les Vxxrrs étant dispensés de neuf en neuf, en redoublant on arriverait au n° 63, et on gagnerait la partie; mais enfin, pour la gagner définitivement, il faut arriver juste au numéro 63.

Qui fera 6, où il y a *Les palissades du pont des Invalides*, payera 1 et se placera au n° 12. — Qui ira au n° 19, où il y a le *Ministère de la Guerre*, payera 2 et attendra que ses partenaires aient joué chacun deux fois. — Qui ira au n° 31, où il y a *Le Mont Valérien*, payera 3 et attendra qu'un autre l'en retire en prenant sa place, puis il ira au numéro qu'occupait celui qui l'en a retiré.

Qui ira au n° 42, où se trouvent les bureaux de l'État-Major, payera 2 et retournera au n° 30.

Qui ira au n° 52, où se trouve la *Prison du Cherche-Midi*, payera 3 et y restera jusqu'à ce qu'il en soit chassé par un autre qui changera de place avec lui. — Qui ira au n° 58, où se trouve la *Mort de la Danse macabre*, payera 3 et recommencera au n° 1. — Qui sera rencontré par l'un des joueurs, payera 3 et prendra la place que celui-ci occupait.

published in *L'Aurore*, September 29, 1899, Zola expresses his happiness to the condemned man's wife:

> They give you back the innocent, the martyr; the husband and the father is given back to his wife, his son, his daughter; my first thought goes toward the family finally reunited, comforted, happy. Notwithstanding my grief as a citizen, my painful indignation, and the continued anguished struggle of just souls, I am with you this blissful minute, mixed with the relief of tears, the minute when you held tightly in your arms the dead come back to life, issued alive and free from the tomb. In spite of all, this day is a great day of victory and rejoicing.

Zola was really one of the greatest contributors to the victory. He was known until then as a great writer; but in the years from 1897 to 1900 he showed that his courage was not inferior to his talent.

However, he will not profit from it. The readers who during that period turned away from his works will not come back to them; although his reputation has increased abroad, the sales of his books decrease. Not only the last

The famous memorandum which Captain Dreyfus was accused of having written

ones are scorned, but also the earlier ones, those of the good period. The Dreyfus case cost him a great deal. He was offered considerable sums of money in England to write about it, but he refused because he did not want to publish articles dealing with what he considered a purely French quarrel in a foreign country. As for the articles he gave to the French newspapers, he never accepted payment for them. He was repulsed by the thought of mixing money in any way with the cause of justice.

Barrès said to Zola: "The Alps are between you and me." For people went so far as to blame Zola for having an Italian father; what was he not accused of, in fact, in the "well-meaning" circles! But it is enough, to judge the various attitudes, to refer to some statements by Barrès, speaking about Dreyfus during the second trial: "In order to get to his followers, we must run him through. Let us go to it, this weak obstacle must not encumber my country's destiny." It is a strange destiny to be bound to such a bad cause; it is a singular conception of his country to claim that it is threatened by the truth, by the reparation of an injustice. . . .

Among the working class, on the contrary, the change of mind is completely in favor of Zola. He had been accused of slandering the workers when he published *The Dram-shop* and *Germinal*. But in 1901, certain workers' associations organize a banquet to celebrate the publication of *Labor (Travail)*.

John Labusquière, a disciple of Fourier, will preside at the banquet instead of Zola, who declines in these terms:

> I must thank you for the great pleasure you have given me and the great honor you have done me by agreeing to preside at the banquet with which the disciples of Fourier and of the labor associations wish to celebrate the publication of my novel, *Labor*.
>
> If I am not with you today, it is because I thought it more modest and more logical that I should not be there. *I* am not important, nor even my work; what you are celebrating is the effort toward more justice, the good fight for man's happiness; and I am with all of you. Is it not enough that my thoughts be yours?
>
> Our hopes are high, the future is the realm of dreams. But, beginning today, one thing is certain, which everything indicates and proves: the future of society is in the reorganization of labor, and from that reorganization alone will come, at

last, a just distribution of wealth. Fourier was the brilliant harbinger of that truth. All I did was to take it up again, and, whatever the road, the City of Peace is at the end of it.

Obviously the Zola of 1901 is no longer the same man who, in his essay on Hugo about fifteen years before, blamed the poet for his utopian views: "Likewise his striking the priests and the kings with his thunderbolts, while he extolled the ideal brotherhood of the people, will not keep the people from devouring one another in the ensuing centuries."

On August 8, 1902, Zola writes to Alfred Bruneau that he has just finished *Truth (Vérité)* which is a fictionalization of the Dreyfus case:

> My dear friend, I have finally finished *Truth* which for a year demanded a good deal from me. The work is at least as long as *Fecundity,* and in it are such a diversity of characters, such an mass of facts, that my work has never demanded a stricter discipline from me. I come out of it quite lively however, and my head alone needs rest.

And he ends with these words: "All three of you will come back to us in radiant health, and that is what is needed to conquer destiny."

It will not be long, however, before he will be struck by fate himself.

> à Émile Zola
>
> en témoignage de ma vive admiration, de ma grande reconnaissance et de ma profonde affection
>
> A Dreyfus

Alfred Dreyfus's dedication on a copy of *Five Years of My Life*

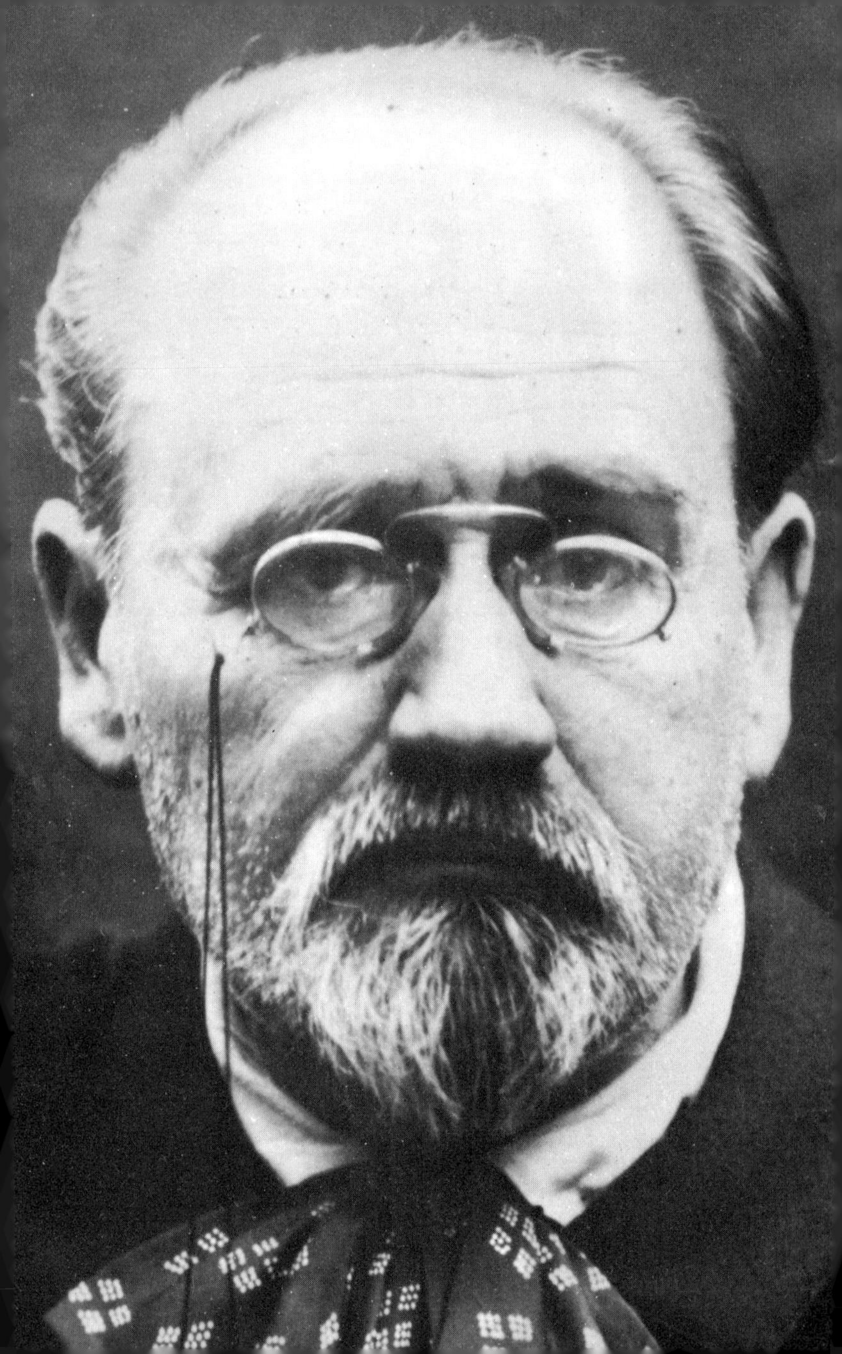

Death

The two Goncourt brothers, Flaubert, Alphonse Daudet, Maupassant are dead. Then it is Paul Alexis' turn to go. On August 6, 1901, Zola expressed his bereavment thus:

> Thank you, my dear Seménoff, for your letter about dear Alexis' death. I find all your goodness of heart in it. I am very sad, it is true, for it is once more a part of my life that goes away. Little by little I alone am left of our literary group.

But he is himself close to his end. The first three *Gospels* have just been published; he will not have time to write the last one, *Justice*.

On September 29, 1902, he comes to Paris to spend the winter. The apartment, empty for several months, is damp; a fire is lighted in the fireplace, then Zola and his wife eat a copious meal and go to bed.

Mme. Zola gets up in the middle of the night; her head feels heavy; she is extremely tired. She goes into the bathroom where she vomits; she stays there a long time, waiting to regain her strength. When she comes back into the bedroom, her husband has just woken up; he too is feeling ill, he thinks it is an attack of indigestion. He gets up and falls on the floor. Mme. Zola tries to reach the bell to call the servants, but she does not have the strength and faints on the bed where she was leaning.

About nine o'clock in the morning, the worried servants decide to open the door of the room. Émile Zola is dead; his wife is taken to a clinic. The author was sixty-two years old; he died without knowing it, asphyxiated.

His funeral took place Sunday, October 5, in the midst of an enormous crowd. At the Montmartre cemetery Anatole France made a speech which he ended with these words:

> Let us not pity him for having endured and suffered. Let us envy him. Rising above the most prodigious heap of insults that stupidity, ignorance and malice have ever raised, his glory reaches inaccessible heights.
>
> Let us envy him: he has done honor to his fatherland and to the world with his enormous work and a great deed. Let us envy him; his destiny and his heart afforded him the best lot in life: he was a moment of human conscience.

Six years later, on June 6, 1908, Zola's ashes were placed in the Panthéon, and people fought again as in the time of the Dreyfus affair. Zola's power and pugnacity were such that they extended beyond death.

About 1901

ÉMILE ZOLA

MES HAINES

CAUSERIES

LITTÉRAIRES ET ARTISTIQUES

> Si vous me demandez ce que je viens faire en ce monde, moi artiste, je vous répondrai : « Je viens vivre tout haut. »

PARIS

ACHILLE FAURE, LIBRAIRE-ÉDITEUR

23, BOULEVARD SAINT-MARTIN, 23

1866

Zola: Simple and Complex

The general pattern of Zola's existence, his highly assured air, do not prevent some peculiarities and contradictions from appearing here and there in his work. To be sure the part fantasy and doubt play are rather small in this life totally devoted to work and based, it would seem, on quiet certainties. As soon as Zola found his direction, he started on it resolutely with a kind of impatience and without ever straying from it. But no life, however straight it may appear, is without its meanderings, conspicuous or hidden.

The fact that until the age of twenty-one, Émile Zola recoils from reality – from what he calls reality – and the fact that he declares that it is horrible, are surely fascinating in the man who will become the leader of the naturalistic school; we should perhaps not attach more importance to his outlook at that time than to simple growing pains. No work of any value came of it, which undoubtedly proves that the real Zola was not there.

More important is his attack on Proudhon in 1866. Émile Zola is twenty-six when he publishes his collection of articles and essays entitled *My Hatreds (Mes Haines)*. At this time he is aware of his personality, he has already made his profession

of faith in naturalism; he is on the verge of writing *Thérèse Raquin*, of conceiving *The Rougon-Macquart* series. He knows what he wants, what he likes and what he hates. He has put down his stakes; he has chosen his gods. In *My Hatreds* he puts into practice the advice which he will give Théodore Duret in 1870: "To say good things about those whom we love is not enough; we must say evil things about those whom we hate."
And here is his praise of hatred:

> Hatred is holy. It is the indignation of stout and powerful hearts, the militant disdain of those who are angered by mediocrity and stupidity. To hate is to love; it is to feel one's soul warm and generous; it is to live fully, despising the shameful and the inane.
> Hatred relieves, hatred does justice, hatred makes us bigger. ... If I am worth anything today, it is because I am alone and I hate.
> I hate the weak nobodies; they bother me.

He goes as far as to say: "I prefer, like Stendhal, a scoundrel to an idiot. . . . Mediocre people must all be thrown into the Place de Grève to be executed. I hate them."
He also asserts: "I do not have much concern for beauty nor perfection. I do not care about the great eras. I am concerned only with life, struggle and fever. I am at ease among my own generation."
That book, however, is far from expressing the dogmatism found in *The Experimental Novel*. It contains nothing but spontaneous impressions, outbursts of the heart and the mind: without affectation, without stiff academic theories, Zola expresses what he thinks of various problems. Two essays in the book, one on a posthumous work of Proudhon, the other where he speaks incidentally of Pascal, reveal a rather unexpected Zola.
Criticizing *The Principle of Art and its Social Destination*, the young author claims to be passionately individualistic. Against Proudhon, who considers art an object of pleasure or of social utility, the indignant Zola demands – and in what tones! – absolute freedom for the artist; he refuses servitude, however it be colored. He knows only one command: that of creating, free of any party or class instructions; in his eyes only one faithfulness is valid, that of the artist toward his work,

without any utilitarian considerations. This he expresses rather violently:

> Your community of interests and your uniformity nauseate us. We produce style and art with our flesh and our soul; we are lovers of life, we give you each day a little of our existence. We are in no one's service, and we refuse to be in yours.

He writes this magnificent statement: "If you ask me what I come to do on this earth, I an artist, I shall answer you: 'I come to live aloud.'"

He claims absolute individualism: "In one word, I am completely opposed to Proudhon: he wants art to be the product of the nation, I demand that it be the product of the individual."

A little later he insists again: "My own art is, on the contrary, a negation of society, an affirmation of the individual, apart from all rules and all social necessities."

It is a passionate plea, and undoubtedly this cry of alarm has for us today a rather prophetic sound. Ahead of his time by almost a century, Zola attacks the abuse of power in which some people are ready to indulge, people who, with cries of "Long live freedom!," suppress freedom in darkness.

In his pages devoted to the Goncourts' novel, *Germinie Lacerteux,* Zola makes this surprising admission: "My taste, if you like, is depraved; I like strongly spiced literary stews, decadent works where a sickly sensitivity replaces the radiant health of classical periods.

Can we imagine two human beings more different than Zola and Pascal? Yet here is how the naturalistic novelist reacts upon reading the *Pensées*:

> At the risk of seeming to have a mediocre intelligence, I should like to say in two words the impression that a page of Pascal has always made on me. I have been frightened by my own lack of belief, and even more so by his beliefs; he has given me cold sweats when he has shown me the horrors of my doubt, and yet I would not have traded my shivers for the shivers of his faith. Pascal proves my own misery to me without convincing me that I should share his. I remain myself through all this, although I am disturbed and my soul bleeds.

Do we not find the same attitude, the same disturbance, profound but incapable of changing his convictions, in Zola's choice of Lazarus' resurrection as the theme of a "lyrical comedy in one act?" Lazarus' mother, his wife and his child have begged Jesus to give him back to them; but the man who has risen from the dead does not wish any longer to live....

> That long dark sleep, that great dreamless sleep was so good, O Jesus! I had never known the sweetness of absolute rest; it can be found only in the tomb. At last I was sleeping, I was resting in the infinite delights of night and silence.
>
> Nothing came from the earth, neither the echo of a noise nor the shiver of daylight. And I was motionless, ah, in eternal immobility, in an endless beatitude, so divine, in the total absence of the world.
>
> O Master, why have you awakened me? Why so cruelly tear the poor dead away from the joy of eternal sleep?...
>
> JESUS. Poor man, your friends, your family wanted it so, for their own happiness. You will live again.
>
> LAZARUS. Live again, oh no, oh no! Have I not settled with pain my frightful debt to life? I was born without knowing why, I lived without knowing how; and you would make me pay double, you would condemn me to begin again my time of suffering on this grief-hidden earth!
>
> What inexpiable sin have I committed to deserve such punishment from you? To live again, alas! To feel oneself die a little every day in one's own flesh; to have intelligence only to doubt; to have will only to be will-less; to be tender only to weep over the sorrows of my heart!
>
> And it was all over; I had crossed death's threshold, that moment so horrible that it is enough to poison one's entire life. I had felt the perspiration of agony soaking me, my blood running out of my limbs, and breath escaping in the last rattle. And you wish me to experience this distress twice, to die twice, and to make my misery worse than that of all men. Oh, Master, no! No!
>
> THE MOTHER. Lazarus, do you not know me? I am your mother, and my side trembled with joy when I saw you alive, erect. What happiness it is to have you again, to keep you once more! Come, I shall lead you; I shall wait on you, just as in the old days, when you were small.
>
> LAZARUS. No, no, mother; love me enough to leave me the

only happiness. What renewed grief it would be if I lost you again. Soon you will join me, and you will see how good it is, how good. When you have known the delights of this sleep, there is not a comparable pleasure on earth.

THE WIFE. And what about me, Lazarus? Me, your wife who sighs after your embraces, and who has been shivering here ever since the sound of your voice touched my neck like the June wind. Do you not want to know me any more and make me happy?

LAZARUS. O wife, dear wife, I am only an unfaithful husband who has slept in another woman's bed, the sweetest, the most tempting, the most unforgettable one. I have slept with death, the eternal mistress, and it was so good, so good to sleep in her arms of silence and darkness, that my lips are no longer made for your living lips.

THE CHILD. And me, father, your child, are you going to forget me? You used to hold my hand; you took me along the roads. Are you going to leave me all alone? And you used to tell me every morning that I should love life.

LAZARUS. Oh, I have loved life with all my heart, all my strength. I lived the way we love. I have given all of me to the joy of being. And that is the way you will live, my child – by continuing my work. Your mother is here; she will guide you. As for me, I finished my task; I lay down in the evening, and no one had the right to wake me out of my sleep, my good sleep.

JESUS. You do not want to live again then, my brother, poor man who makes me weep?

LAZARUS. No, no! Do not inflict upon me the torment of living twice, so dreadful a torment that you have not yet condemned any man to it. I have always loved you and served you, O Master; do not set me as the greatest example of what your anger can do, that anger which would frighten generations.

THE CHILD. Father, have you seen Heaven? Is that why you leave us?

THE WIFE. What superhuman ideas call you back to paradise?

THE MOTHER. Tell us what you have seen, on the other side of the wall, from where nobody ever comes back?

LAZARUS. Nothing, nothing, nothing. I slept. The dark immensity, the infinitely silent. But if you only knew how good it is to be no more, to sleep in the void of everything!

O Master, if you can, I beg you to perform that other great miracle which would make me lie again in this tomb, and without pain, sleep again my eternal interrupted sleep.

O my mother, my wife, my child, my friends, if you love me, see to it that justice is done. Beg Jesus to give me back to the sweet death from whom no one had the right to take me away.

The Mother. Work this one more miracle. I love my son enough to want only his happiness; and let him sleep waiting for me, since he knows where happiness is!

The Wife. I also implore you, work this miracle. The memory of our kisses will be warmer than this pale ghost from the tomb. And I shall be happy if he is happy.

The Child. My father is tired; work this miracle that he go back to sleep painlessly. Life will not end, I am here to continue it.

The Chorus. Painlessly we implore you. Lazarus was not suffering any more; he must not suffer again. Work this miracle, and let Lazarus go back to sleep painlessly.

Jesus. Yes, yes, painlessly, this time, poor Lazarus. You wanted it, and you have heard; you know now. After life's passion, death is the great comfort. To force him to live again made my stern heart bleed for him. And it is wise, it is just, it is good that he go back to sleep.

Lazarus. Thank you, O Jesus!

(He walks back into the tomb.)

Jesus. Lazarus, go back to sleep!

(Lazarus lies down.)

Lazarus, go back to sleep!

Lazarus (in a weak voice). What comfort! Thank you, O Jesus!

Jesus. Lazarus, go back to sleep!

Lazarus (weaker and weaker). The dark immensity, the infinite silence, thank you, O Jesus!

(His voice dies out.)

Jesus. Lazarus, go back to sleep!

(A long silence.)

Replace the stone.

(The three men replace the stone on the tomb.)

Ah, poor human creature, creature of suffering and misery, sleep, sleep now, forever happy, unto eternity.

ALL. Ah, poor Lazarus, poor tired man, broken by suffering and misery, sleep, sleep now, forever happy, unto eternity.

(Médan, January 1, 1894.)

We probably should assign a large part of what is hard to account for in Zola to the attraction he feels toward religious objects. On his desk was an ivory crucifix, a chalice, a host container, a small case containing a picture of the Virgin. From Lourdes he had brought back a large rosary.

Émile Zola on his death bed

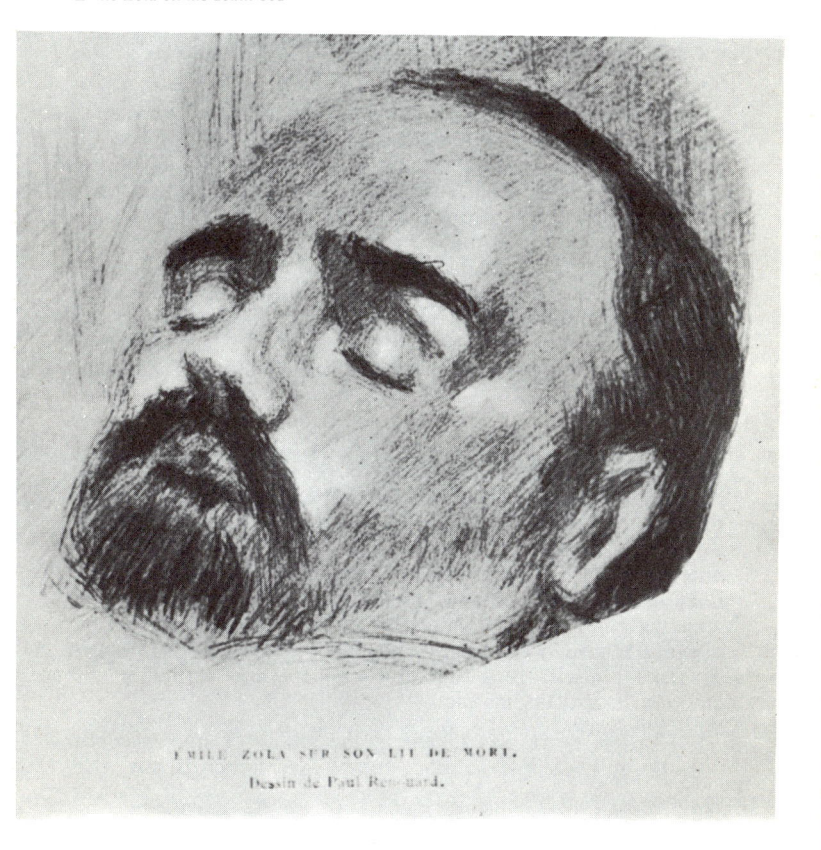

It is a constant source of amazement to me that Zola kept most of these objects before his eyes, within reach. Nothing was more foreign to him than idolatry. He considered himself a man of science as much as a writer; entirely taken by the social, he denied the supernatural; he had refused once and for all to turn to metaphysics, so what peculiar attraction could he find in these tokens of a faith so completely alien to him? Was he simply sensitive to the poetry of these religious objects, or did he assert his own agnosticism by means of these signs of what was for him superstition?

It is to be feared that Zola, who was rather stingy with intimate information, has taken with him the only valid answer to those questions. But we cannot dismiss this aspect of him without juxtaposing it to that which led him to create in his novels so many priests, all of them evil or mediocre.

And do we not discover another aspect of Zola's complexity in his outlook on his own work – on the fame which it affords him, and on the crushing amount of work which he devotes to it day after day? Zola's extraordinary self-assurance seems secretly haunted by a profound doubt, in the face of which his success is no proof and his very existence absurd.

To be sure it would be rather hasty to conclude that the author's repeated assertions (work constituting his greatest and perhaps his unique happiness) are no more than defensive and a stiffening of his will against the very doubt which constantly threatens him. Against the oversimplified picture of Zola "all cast in a simple mold," we see little use in opposing the equally oversimplified one of Zola torn apart, tormented, and forever having to keep a hold on himself. But in the following lines, taken from *The Masterpiece (L'Oeuvre)* – where Zola presents himself under the guise of Sandoz, and describes Cézanne through the figure of Claude – do we not see a suggestion that, in spite of everything, his doubt was deeply rooted, and that only an act of faith, extreme and as vehement as a revolt, could hold it in check? In any case, it is interesting to offer the amazing confidence of Sandoz as a contrast to the attitude he displayed through Lazarus. The sudden reversal through which he frees himself from that attitude here and surmounts his emotion is also fascinating:

"Listen; work has taken up the whole of my existence. Little by little, it has robbed me of my mother, of my wife,

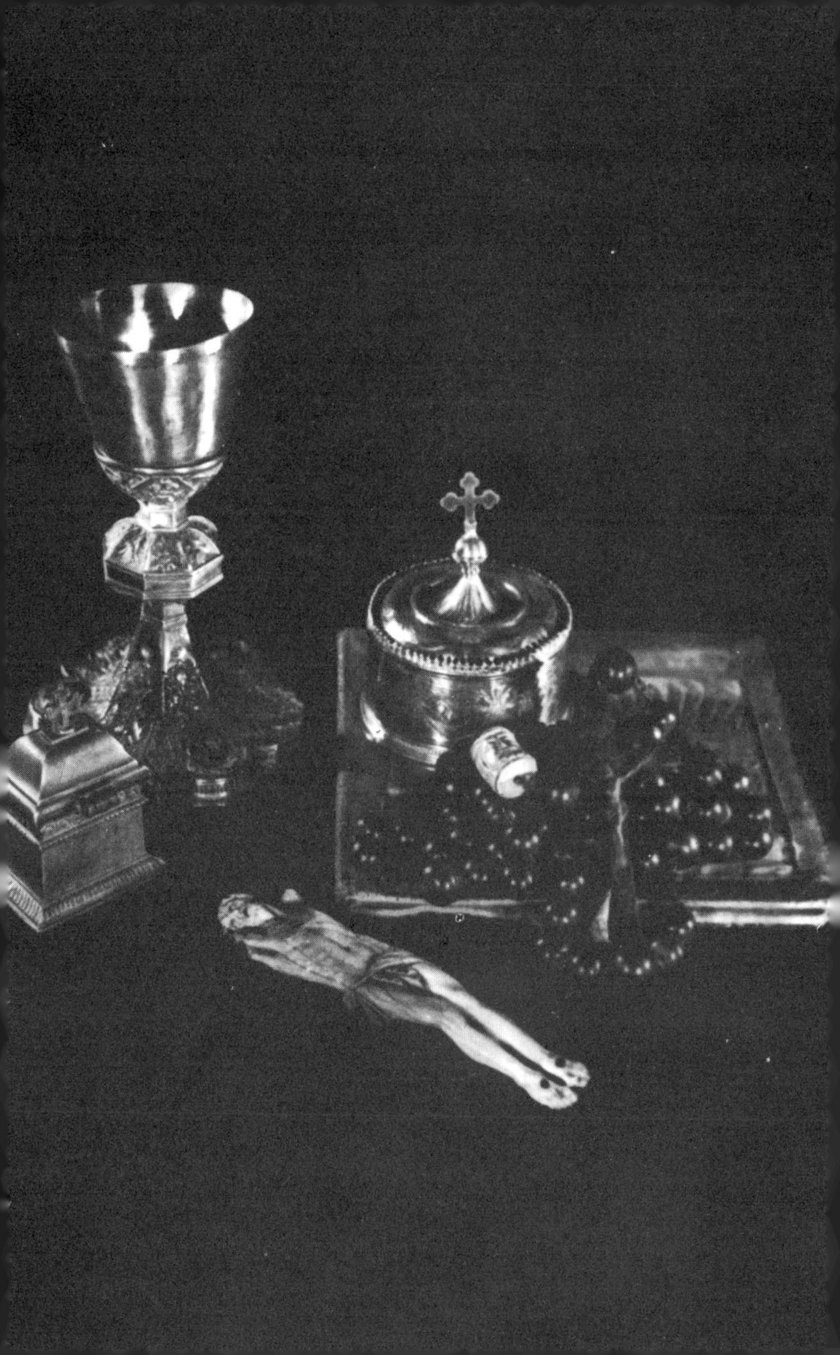

of everything I love. It is like a germ thrown into the cranium, which feeds on the brain, finds its way into the trunk and limbs, and gnaws up the whole of the body. The moment I jump out of bed of a morning, work clutches hold of me, rivets me to my desk without leaving me time to get a breath of fresh air; then it pursues me at luncheon – I audibly chew my sentences with my bread. Next it accompanies me when I go out, comes back with me and dines off the same plate as myself; lies down with me on my pillow, so utterly pitiless that I am never able to set the book in hand on one side; indeed, its growth continues even in the depth of my sleep. And nothing outside of it exists for me. True, I go upstairs to embrace my mother, but in so absent-minded a way, that ten minutes after leaving her I ask myself whether I have really been to wish her good-morning. My poor wife has no husband; I am not with her even when our hands touch. Sometimes I have an acute feeling that I am making their lives very sad, and I feel very remorseful, for happiness is solely composed of kindness, frankness and gaiety in one's home; but how can I escape from the claws of the monster? I at once relapse into the somnambulism of my working hours, into the indifference and moroseness of my fixed idea. If the pages I have written during the morning have been worked off all right, so much the better; if one of them has remained in distress, so much the worse. The household will laugh or cry according to the whim of that all-devouring monster.... There is no chance of a walk in the morning's sun, no chance of running round to a friend's house, or of a mad bout of idleness! My strength of will has gone with the rest; all this has become a habit; I have locked the door of the world behind me, and thrown the key out of the window. There is no longer anything in my den but work and myself – and work will devour me, and then there will be nothing left, nothing at all!

... I say nothing of the jugful of insults that are showered upon one. Instead of annoying, they rather encourage me.... It suffices that a man can say that he has given his life's blood to his work; that he expects neither immediate justice nor serious attention; that he works without hope of any kind, and simply because the love of work beats beneath his skin like his heart, irrespective of any will of his own. If he can do all this, he may die in the effort with the consoling illusion that he will be appreciated one day or other. Ah, if the others only knew how jauntily I bear the weight of their anger. Only there is my own choler, which overwhelms me; I fret that I cannot live for a moment happy. What hours of misery I spend, great heavens, from the very day I begin a novel: During the first chapters there isn't so much trouble. I have plenty of room before me in which to display genius. But afterwards I become distracted, and am never satisfied with the daily task; I condemn the book before it is finished, judging it inferior to its elders; and I torture myself about certain pages, about certain sentences, certain words, so that at last the very commas assume an ugly look, from which I suffer. And when it is finished; – ah, when it is finished, what a relief! Not the enjoyment of the gentleman who exalts himself in the worship of his offspring, but the curse of the labourer who throws down the burden that has been breaking his back. Then, later on, with another book, it all begins afresh; it will always begin afresh, and I shall die under it, furious with myself, exasperated at not having had more talent, enraged at not leaving a "work" more complete, of greater dimensions – books upon books, a pile of mountain height! And at my death I shall feel horrible doubts about the task I may have accomplished, asking myself whether I ought not to have gone to the left when I went to the right, and my last word, my last gasp, will be to recommence the whole over again."

He was thoroughly moved; the words stuck in his throat; he was obliged to draw breath for a moment before delivering himself of this passionate cry in which all his impenitent lyricism took wing:

"Ah, life! a second span of life, who shall give it to me, that work may rob me of it again – that I may die of it once more?"

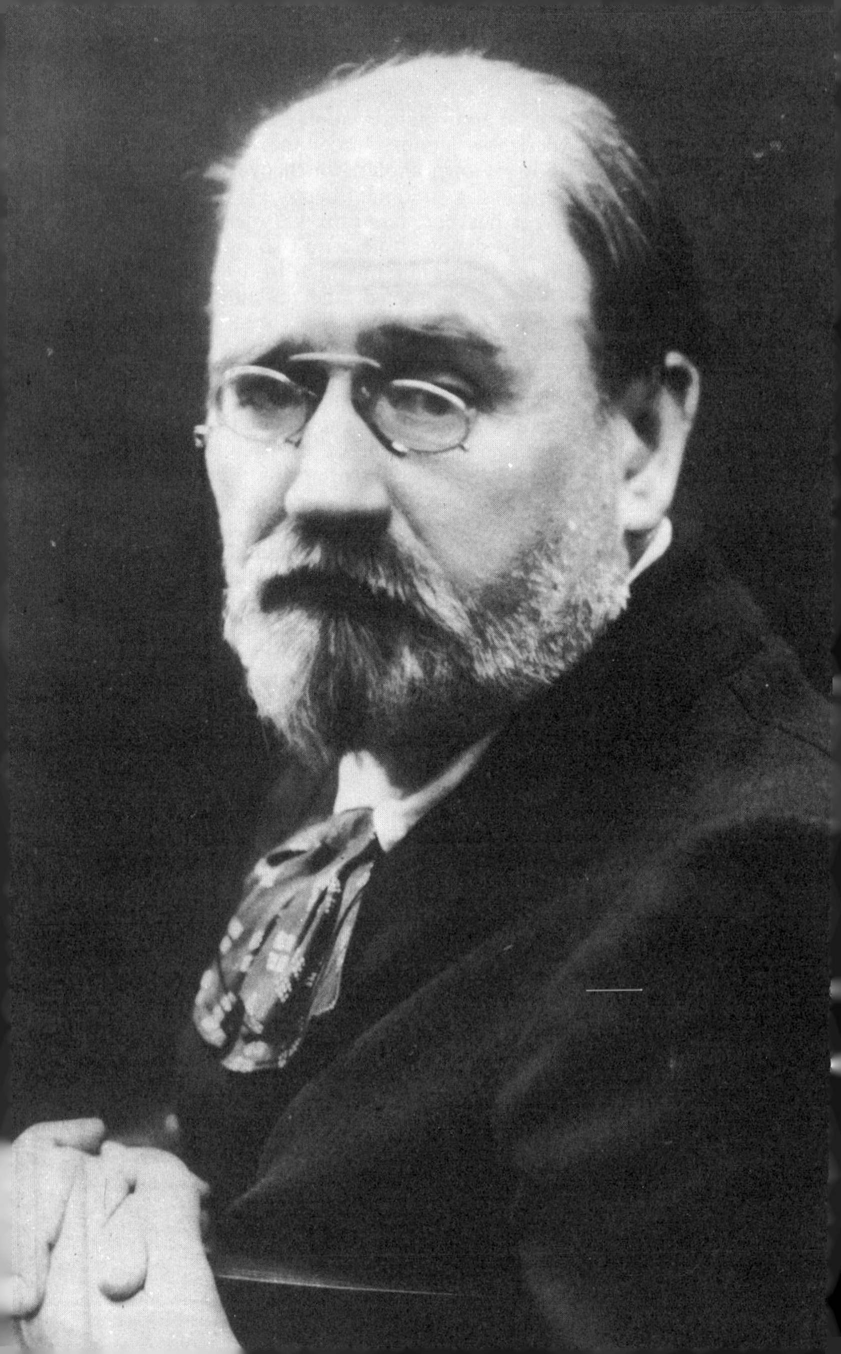

Zola after Death

Zola died in 1902; enough time has elapsed to judge his work, to free it from the fashions of its era, from those reactions to it which could alter its meaning.

This must be recognized: it happens often when an author sets out to produce a huge quantity of work, a great deal is wasted. But the high points of his work now stand out very clearly. I believe it can be said that the reputations of *Thérèse Raquin*, *The Dram-shop*, *Nana*, *Germinal* and *The Human Beast* will not lessen; these novels are worthy of posterity.

As for Zola's influence, it is unquestionable, not only in France but in the literature of the world. There are few modern novelists who do not owe him something, even when they do not know it. Zola has given us the taste for strong reality and the courage to show it. As Nietzsche says, his example has made us "more cynical, but more frank."

Naturalism has been blamed for giving a degrading picture of man, of having caught only the lowest in him, and of showing us, in the guise of reality, traits that belong to the realm of the instinctive and the physiological. And undoubtedly Dostoevsky's greatness lies in the fact that he was able to describe man in his integrity, his complexity, his total truth: body and

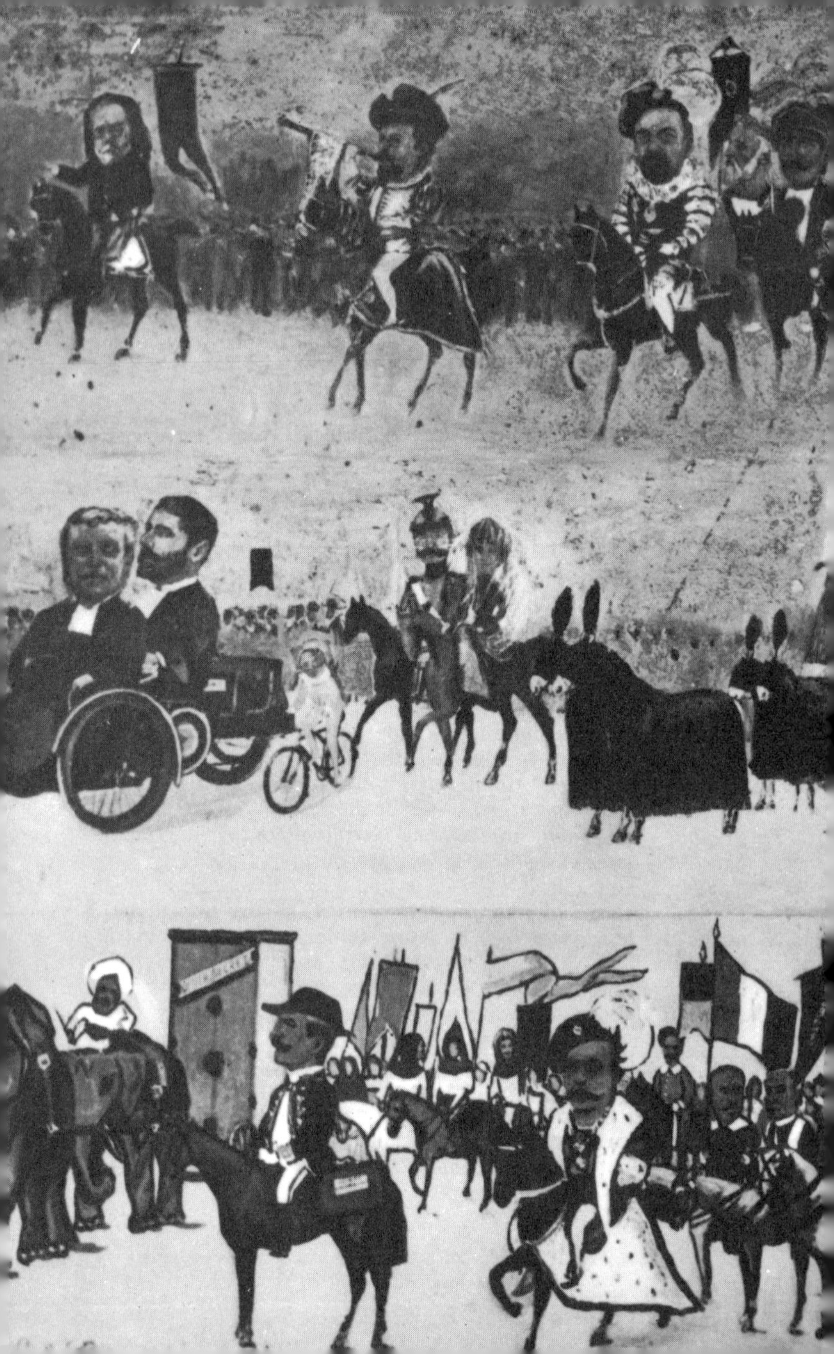

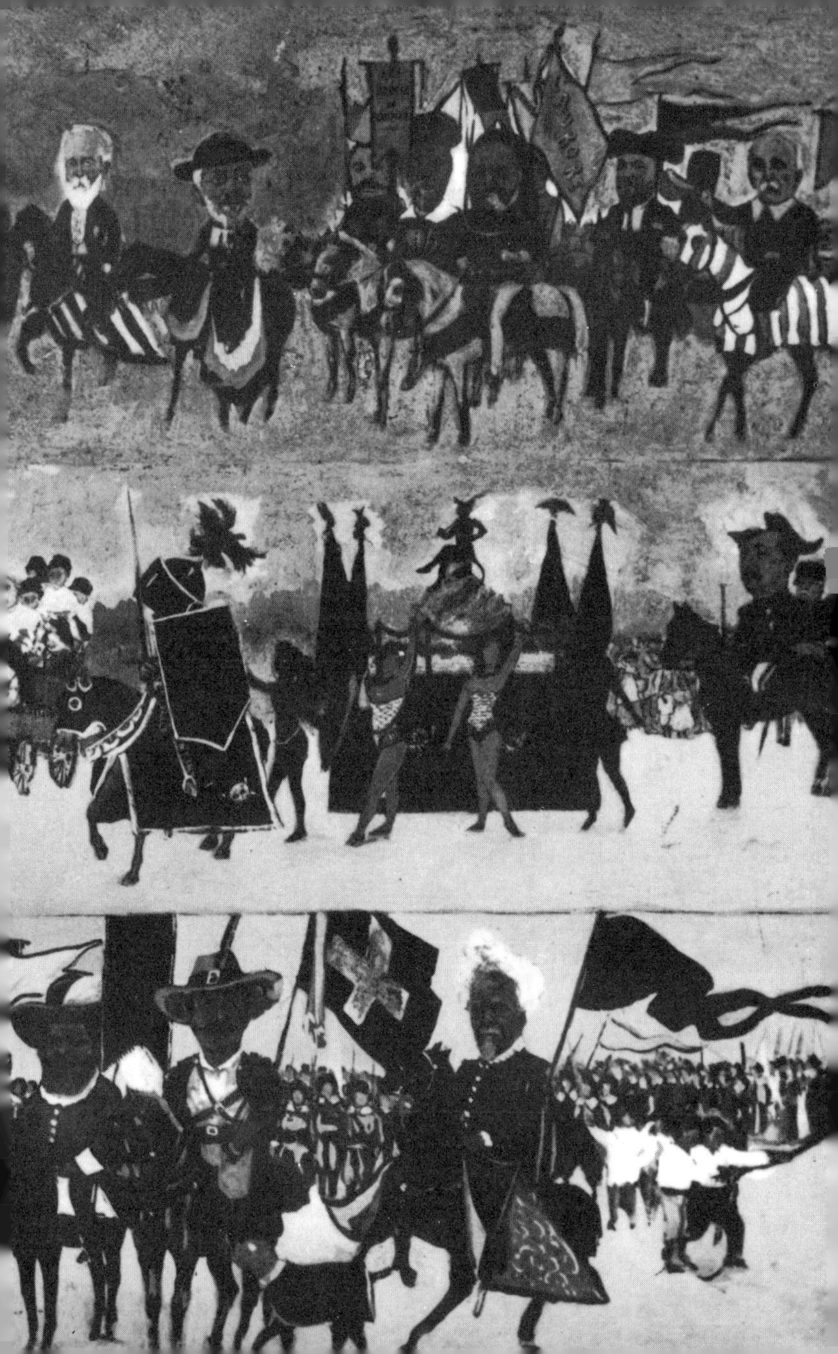

soul. But it seems that in this respect naturalism is less responsible than his founder. Each time Émile Zola applied himself to describing the other aspect of man, he fell into insipidity.... An artist of a rarely equaled force, he must be taken the way he is or else rejected. If he did not give us a new image of man, at least we are in debt to him for having shed light with masterful force on entire masses, something no writer before him had been able to do. And his genius is not limited to the discovery of the model: it was not enough to conceive it, he also had to be able to breathe life into those huge frescoes. The results achieved after him in this field, the failures of the few who tried their luck in the same direction, even when they may have had less ambitious plans, prove sufficiently that the themes tackled by Zola were suited only to an exceptional talent.

Another one of his lessons, and not the least, is a lesson in courage: all that is real is ours and nothing must prevent us from expressing it. We know that dangers threaten this freedom: it must constantly be fought for.

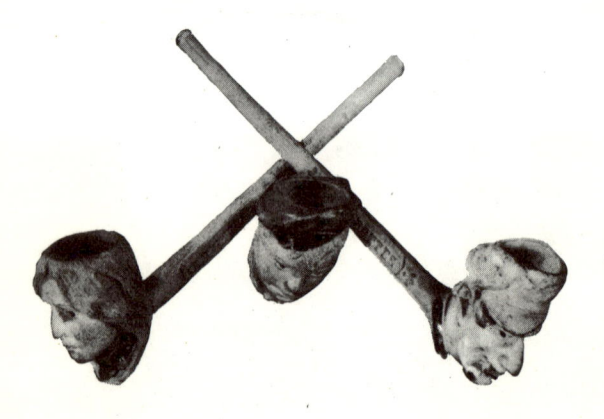

Finally one more point must be emphasized: his work, in its best portions, is infinitely more useful than that of many moralists, and it is probably when Zola was least concerned with helping that he helped the most. He showed the injustice of social inequalities, based only on man's origins.... While the esthetic writers turned their eyes away from the proletarian condition or, even worse, skirted it without seeing it, he devoted a masterpiece to it with *Germinal*.

Zola's sympathy for the people was reciprocated by the people when they understood the profound feelings that moved the author. During Zola's lifetime a kind of folklore appeared taking its themes from his work. Clay pipes represented the principal characters of *The Dram-shop;* dinner plates were decorated with scenes from his books; rings and medallions with his effigy were sold; pens bore his name; statuettes represented Gervaise with her wooden beetle in hand, spanking her rival, in the best wash-house style of *The Dram-shop.* A complete set of naïve and good-natured images also came out of Zola's novels. Today the interest has not lessened; in the libraries, his works are in great demand.

Such recognition was his due, for Zola writes well only about the people; when he moves away from them, his work weakens. He is not an author who looks down at his subject; he is on his model's level, although he is often blind to the dreams and fantasies which are a large part of the worker's mind. But what of it! Nuances and refinement are not his forte, and an athlete cannot be asked to have the grace of a dancer.

As he stands, Zola is enormous; his gigantic stature makes him a phenomenon. He will continue to arouse enthusiasm for a long time to come.

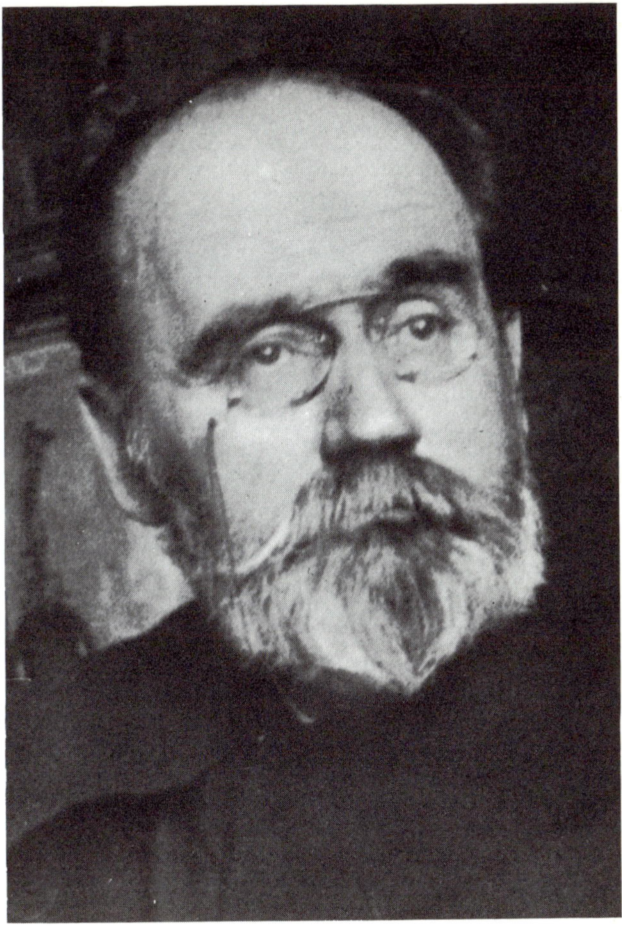

L'observation et l'expérience. Nous autres
romanciers sommes nous des observateurs ou des
expérimentateurs ? Résoudre la question avec
citations

Définition de la méthode expérimentale (22 et 24)
× Différence de l'observateur et de l'expérimentateur (29)
× L'expérience est une observation provoquée (36)
Définition de l'investigateur qui cherche observe etc (38)
× Tout le mécanisme de l'observat. et de l'exp. (40 et 41)
× L'idée première, et le mécanisme de ce qui suit (44)
× Encore un résumé excellent (47)
à prendre très important
Exposé hist. de l'évolution de l'intell. humaine (50)
× Toute la théorie du roman expérimental (54)
L'expérimentateur est le juge d'instruction de la nature (56)
L'idée antérieure et première (58)
Tout repose sur le doute (91)
Il n'y a que des vérités relatives, et dans le roman (96)
× Dans la pratique les hommes font continuellement
des expériences les uns sur les autres (177)   340

Sur l'observation et l'expérience. Sans réplique : 364.
Il discute, puis à prouver la ressemblance et il conclut. L'idéaliste

On dit la médecine est un art et non une science, comme pour le roman. (voir note 10)

Entrée en matière. J'ai parlé souvent de la science dans le roman. On s'est moqué. Je veux nettement arrêter ce qui me paraît être. — Je prends le livre d'un savant et je l'étudie à ce point de vue. *la médecine entre dans la vie réelle.* Je trouve là toutes les questions traitées, pleines d'arguments. Tout a fait définitif, sur la matière. Il n'y a le plus souvent qu'à mettre le mot romancier au lieu du mot médecin (ou autre). Je vais exposer brièvement l'ensemble du livre, car je ne veux pas en suivre l'ordre logique.

Un court exposé du livre de Claude Bernard. Tout résumé brièvement

I. L'observation et l'expérience.
II. Du corps brut, aux corps vivants et au roman.
III. Se rendre maître de la matière. Morale. Utilité. Idéal.
IV. Les médecins sont des artistes. Génie. Science dans le roman.
V. Pas de formules ni de théorie. Pas de philo. Mon novateur. La formule la large

The documents reproduced on pages 174 and 175 are notes taken by Zola for his essay on *The Experimental Novel*. It is interesting to follow his method in this case, from the discovery of Claude Bernard's book, *Introduction to the Study of Experimental Medicine,* to the definitive composition of his own text.

1. Many pencil marks in the book's margin, but almost no annotation.
2. Twelve sheets of notes in pencil, recalling the important ideas in the book, with a few remarks on their application to the novel.
3. Eight sheets of notes in ink, selecting and assembling the preceding notes, at the rate of one per two or three sheets in pencil; once repeated or used in this manner, each note is crossed out in ink (see above, pp. 174-175).
4. On a ninth sheet in ink Zola puts down the ideas which he will set forth in the first four pages of the introduction to his essay, as well as the general plan of that essay, with the five parts it will comprise.
5. Finally here is the text of the first two pages of the introduction, corresponding to the first twelve lines of the sheet on page 175 (the other two pages constitute "a short account of Claude Bernard's book"):

> In my literary essays I have often spoken of the application of the experimental method to the novel and to the drama. The return to nature, the naturalistic evolution which marks the century, little by little drives all the manifestations of human intelligence into the same scientific path. The idea of a literature governed by science is doubtless a surprise, until explained with precision and understood. It seems to me necessary, therefore, to say briefly and to the point what I understand by the experimental novel.
>
> I really only need to adapt, for the experimental method has been established with strength and marvelous clearness by Claude Bernard in his *Introduction à l'Étude de la Médecine Expérimentale*. This work, by a scholar whose authority is unquestioned, will serve me as a solid foundation. The whole question is treated here, and I shall restrict myself to irrefutable arguments and to giving the quotations which may seem necessary to me. This will then be but a compiling of texts, as I intend on all points to intrench myself behind Claude Bernard. It will often be necessary for me only to replace the word "doctor" by the word "novelist," in order to make my meaning clear and to give it the firmness of a scientific truth.
>
> What determined my choice, and made me select the *Introduction* as my foundation, was the fact that medicine, in the eyes of a great number of people, is still an art, as is the novel. Claude Bernard all his life searched and battled to make medicine scientific. In his struggle we see the first feeble attempts of medicine to disengage itself little by little from empiricism,* and to gain, by means of the experimental

---

*) Zola uses empiricism in this essay in the sense of "haphazard observation" in contrast with a scientific experiment undertaken to prove a certain truth.

method, a foothold in the realm of truth. Claude Bernard demonstrates that this method, pursued in the study of inanimate bodies of chemistry and in physics, should be also used in the study of living bodies, in physiology and medicine. I am going to try to prove for my part that if the experimental method leads to the knowledge of physical life, it should also lead to the knowledge of emotional and intellectual life. It is but a question of degree, along the same scale which runs from chemistry to physiology, then from physiology to anthropology and to sociology. The experimental novel is the ultimate goal.

Raymond Poincaré on *The Experimental Novel:*

I could easily believe that M. Zola let his words far outrun his thought, careful as he was to give his idea an appearance of mathematical precision, and eager as he was to find a striking and original formula. He met with incredulity when he advocated physiological observation. He felt this as the goad of a spur and went galloping through theories, moving back and forth from literature to science, breaking down all barriers, and, if it must be said, sometimes raising a few clouds of dust around himself. Therefore let us admire again the moderation he has been able to maintain. And we are happy to note that, having contested not M. Zola's explanation of the literary movement, but rather the *form* of that explanation, we are obliged to pay close attention to everything he says about the characteristics of the modern novel.

Opinions

Octave Mirbeau:

It is easy to account for the hatred which still haunts Zola — in the midst of much admiration, I hasten to say. His great talent is responsible first of all, for most people do not forgive those who are strong; also responsible is the fact that M. Zola made his way through life all by himself. For the mediocre selfishly enjoy imagining that they have something to do with an author's fame, crying in unison: "I discovered him." But, M. Zola discovered himself. He is not the product of a friendship like so many other successes; he did not come out of the usual fame factories. Sustained by the force of his genius alone, by the strength of his courage, he went straight ahead, and came magnificently to the fore. He did not stoop to any concessions, he did not get into any compromises, any alliances, any of the large schemes or petty plots that make up literary life... and here he is.

(*Le Matin*, November 6, 1885.)

ANATOLE FRANCE:

Gentlemen, while we watched this work rise stone by stone, we measured its size with surprise. Some admired, some wondered, some praised, some criticized. Praise and criticism were uttered with the same vehemence. Some at times (I know it from my own experience) criticized the powerful author honestly, it unjustly. Invectives and apologies collided. Meantime, the work continued to grow.

Today we view the colossal form in its entirety, and we recognize also the spirit with which it is filled. It is a spirit of goodness. Zola was good. He had the candor and the simplicity of great souls. He was profoundly moral. He painted vice with a stern and virtuous hand. His apparent pessimism, a somber mood found in more than one of his pages, cannot hide a real optimism, an obstinate faith in the progress of intelligence and justice. In his novels, which are social essays, he hunted with a vigorous hatred through an idle and frivolous society, a base and pernicious aristocracy; he fought the evil of his time: the power of money. A democrat, he never flattered the people, and he tried to show them that ignorance is servitude, and the dangers of alcohol that leaves them the dulled and defenseless victims of all kinds of oppression, misery, and shame. He fought social evils wherever he met them. Such were his hatreds. In his last books he showed plainly his fervent love of humanity. He tried to foresee a better society.

He wished that an ever-increasing number of men would find happiness on earth. He put his hopes in the intellect and in science. He looked to the new force, the machine, for the progressive emancipation of laboring humanity.

This sincere realist was an ardent idealist. Only Tolstoy's work is comparable in scope to his. They are two vast, ideal cities built by the lyre at each extremity of European thought. They are both generous and peace-loving. But Tolstoy's city is the city of resignation. Zola's is the city of labor.

(Address on Zola's tomb — *Pages libres*, Oct. 18, 1902.)

HENRI BARBUSSE:

He was not refined. He was nobly common, with an appetite for the palpable and the concrete, gifted with an acuteness as gigantic as himself, full of good sense and clarity, wedded to harsh and simplified methods of work, viewing the populous site of growing Industry and the tumultuous equipment of big business with the eye of a contractor rather than of an encyclopedist, brimming over with vitality, health, and obstinacy. And he was afraid of nothing. "So much the worse for us," cried a contemporary, "if we've got a man who is terrified by nothing!"

He was not a scholar, having had only a rough general education. He did not in the least resemble the intellectual who, after a survey of knowledge, makes a minute investigation, and finally decides upon a doctrine: the intellectual whom Taine, who was so clever at seeing the mote in the eyes of others, reproached for ordering a system as one orders a suit of clothes.

He was not a dialectician. He fought rather than discussed.

Octave Mirbeau's answer to an inquiry by *L'Aurore* (November, 1898)

He was belligerent rather than ambitious. He advanced in a straight line because his weight kept him on the rails.

He proved that he himself was a movement, by advancing. As he proceeded he took on those ideas which were in line with his progress and with the task he was carrying out. Everything that defined, illuminated, coordinated in its various parts, the objective towards which this mighty man advanced gropingly, he seized and assimilated.

(*Zola*, pp. 250-251.)

JULES LEMAITRE:

About *Germinal*:

I do not believe that anyone has ever made such large masses live and move about in any other novel. At time they crawl like an anthill; at other times they are swept at a dizzying pace by an onrush of blind instincts. With his robust patience, his dull brutality, the breadth of his inspiration, the poet unfolds a series of vast and pitiful tableaux composed of monochromic details that pile up and up, rise and sprawl like a high tide: a day in the mine, a day in the tenements, a rebel meeting at night in a clearing, the angry march of three thousand miserable people in the plains, the impact of that mob against the soldiers, ten days of agony in the flooded pit...

M. Zola has rendered magnificently the fatal, the blind, the impersonal, the irresistible character of a drama of this sort, the contagion of mob anger, the collective soul of the people, violent and easily enraged.

(*Revue Politique et Litteraire*, March 14, 1885.)

JULES ROMAINS:

Zola's claims to fame are many. It is commonplace to praise his power of construction; but if the praise is commonplace, the reason for it is not. Since the completion of *The Rougon-Macquart*, almost a half century later, we have learned how rare the genius for construction is, how few great architects there are in literature and elsewhere. We have seen an abundance of clever but small works. More than one, while capturing the precarious favors of the public, found a way to be small without being successfully done. The architect had dreamed of only a kiosk, but he had not even had the strength to make it stand up. Others' works were more ambitious, tried to organize vaster material. But if they were more ambitious, they served to show us, to make more tangible for us, the difficulties inherent in large undertakings. Disconcerted by too much material, or using too little, or offering too limited a view, these apprentices force us to return to Zola, as well as to Hugo. We seek their strength and their ability to encompass the enormity of life.

(*Zola and his example*, 1935.)

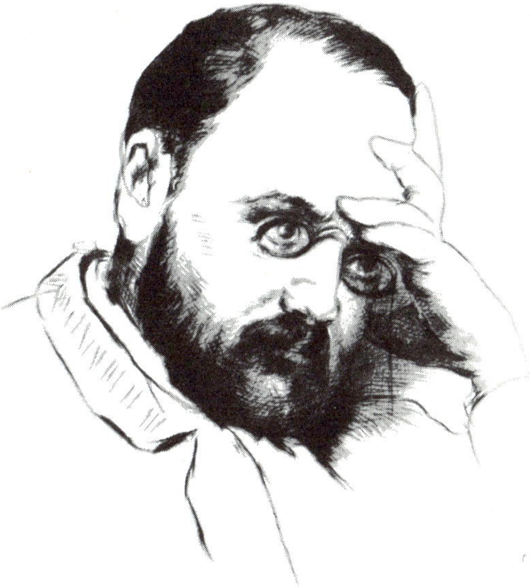

Chronology

1840 April 2: Birth of Zola in Paris.
1847 Death of François Zola.
1850 Dr. Lucas: *Philosophical and Physiological Treatise of Natural Heredity.*
1858 Mme. Zola and her son leave Aix-en-Provence for Paris.
1860 April: Customs Clerk.
1862 February: Clerk, then publicity chief at Hachette's. Naturalization.
1863 Zola's marriage.
1864 October: Publication of the first book, *Tales for Ninon.*
1865 Claude Bernard: *Introduction to the Study of Experimental Medicine.*
1867 May 24: Manet exhibition.
1870 July 13: Dispatch from Ems. September 4: Fall of the Empire and proclamation of the Republic.
1871 March 18: The Paris Commune.
1877 Zola settles at Médan.
1890 Zola refuses to be a candidate for deputy in the fifth ward.
1894 October 15: Dreyfus' arrest. December 22: Deportation to Devil's Island.
1897 December: Zola publishes his first article about the case, in the *Figaro.*
1898 January 13: Publication in *L'Aurore* of the letter to Félix Faure ("I accuse"). February 23: Zola is condemned to one year in prison and fined 3,000 francs. July 18: He leaves for England.
1899 June 5: Zola's return to France. Dreyfus is freed.
1902 September 29: Zola's death in Paris.
1908 June 6: Transfer of Zola's ashes to the Panthéon.

Bibliography

1864 *Tales for Ninon.*
1866 *Claude's Confession.*
1866 *My Hatreds.* (Talks on literature and art.)
1866 *My Salon.* (A collection of articles.)
1866 *A Dead Woman's Wish.*
1867 *Édouard Manet.* (Biographical and critical study.)
1867 *The Mysteries of Marseille.*
1868 *Madeleine Férat.*
1868 *Thérèse Raquin.*
1871 *The Rougon's Luck* (Vol. I of the R.-M.).
1871 *The Quarry* (Vol. II).
1873 *The Bowels of Paris* (Vol. III).
1874 *The Conquest of Plassans* (Vol. IV).
1874 *The Blacksmith.*
1874 *The Rabourdin Heirs.* (Comedy in 3 acts.)
1874 *New Tales for Ninon.*
1875 *Abbé Mouret's Transgression* (Vol. V).
1876 *His Excellency Eugène Rougon* (Vol. VI).
1877 *The Dram-shop* (Vol. VII).
1878 *Theatre: Thérèse Raquin; The Rabourdin Heirs; The Rosebud.*
1879 *The Republic and Literature.* (A collection of articles.)
1880 *Nana* (Vol. IX).
1880 *The Experimental Novel.* Letter to the Youth; Naturalism in the Theatre; Money in Literature; The Novel; The Republic and Literature.

1880 *Evenings at Médan.*

1881 *Literary Documents, Studies and Portraits:* Chateaubriand, Victor Hugo, Alfred de Musset, Th. Gautier. The Contemporary Poets. Morality in Literature.

1881 *Naturalism in the Theatre.* Theories and exemples. (A collection of articles.)

1881 *Our Playwrights.* (A collection of articles.)

1881 *The Naturalistic Novelists:* Balzac, Stendhal, Gustave Flaubert, Edmond and Jules de Goncourt, Alphonse Daudet. The Contemporary Novelists.

1882 *The Boarding House* (Vol. X).

1882 *A Campaign (1880-1881).* (A collection of articles.)

1883 *The Ladies' Paradise* (Vol. XI).

1883 *Captain Burle.* How we die. For a night of love. In the fields. The fair at Coqueville. The flood.

1884 *The Joy of Life* (Vol. XII).

1884 *Naïs Micoulin.* Nantes. Olivier Bécaille's death. Madame Neigeon. M. Chabre's seashells. Jacques Damour.

1884 *Theatre.* Three plays adapted from novels by William Busnach, each preceded by a preface by Émile Zola: *The Dram-shop, Nana, The Boarding House.*

1885 *Germinal* (Vol. XIII).

1886 *The Masterpiece* (Vol. XIV).

1887 *Renée.* Five act play with a preface by the author. (Play adapted from *The Quarry.*)

1887 *The Earth* (Vol. XV).

1888 *The Dream* (Vol. XVI).

1890 *The Human Beast* (Vol. XVII).

1891 *Money* (Vol. XVIII).

1891 *The Dream.* Lyrical drama in 4 acts and 8 scenes, from the novel by Émile Zola. Poem by Louis Gallet, music by Alfred Bruneau.

1892 *The Downfall* (Vol. XIX).

1893 *Doctor Pascal* (Vol. XX).

1893 *The Attack on the Mill.* Lyrical drama in 4 acts. Poem by Louis Gallet, music by Alfred Bruneau.

1894 *Lourdes* (The Three Cities).

1896 *Rome* (The Three Cities).

1897 *Letter to the Youth* (The Dreyfus Case).

1897 *Messidor.* Lyrical drama in 4 acts and 5 scenes. Poem by Émile Zola, music by Alfred Bruneau.

1897 *New Campaign (1896).* (A collection of articles.)

1898 *Letter to France* (Dreyfus Case).

1898 *"I accuse."* Letter published January 13, 1898, in the newspaper *L'Aurore.* Published as a pamphlet under the title: *The Dreyfus Affair,* letter to M. Félix Faure, President of the Republic.

PRIME DU CORSAIRE

UN
DUEL SOCIAL

PAR

AGRIPPA

PREMIÈRE PARTIE

PARIS
AUX BUREAUX DU CORSAIRE
2, RUE DE MULHOUSE, 2
1873

"*A Social Duel*" does not appear in our bibliography, although that title conceals *The Mysteries of Marseille*, and "Agrippa" is none other than Zola himself

MESSIDOR

Drame
Lyrique

Emile Zola

Alfred Bruneau

1898 *Paris* (The Three Cities).
1899 *Fecundity* (The Four Gospels).
1901 *The Hurricane.* Lyrical drama in 4 acts. Poem by Émile Zola. Music by Alfred Bruneau.
1901 *Labor* (The Four Gospels).
1901 *Truth on the march* (Dreyfus Case).

Posthumous Publications:

1903 *Truth* (The Four Gospels).
1905 *The Child-King.* Lyrical comedy in 5 acts. Music by Alfred Bruneau.
1907 *Correspondence:* Letters of his youth.
1907 *Naïs Micoulin.* Lyrical drama in 2 acts taken from the short story. Poem and music by Alfred Bruneau.
1908 *Correspondence:* Letters and The Arts.
1916 *The Four Days.* Lyrical tale in 4 acts and 5 scenes after Émile Zola. Poem and music Alfred Bruneau.
1921 *Lyrical Poems:* Messidor, The Hurricane, The Child-King, Hairy Violaine, Sylvanire, Lazarus.

Studies of Zola's Life and Work

The following work is an invaluable help in the study of Zola:

Hemmings, F. W. J., *Émile Zola* (Oxford: The Clarendon Press, 1953).

It contains a very extensive bibliography, including a complete list of all of Zola's published works (excluding pamphlets) with the dates of appearance, grouped under convenient headings. It also carries a list of manuscript and uncollected material, and a very large number of titles of studies, essays, articles on Zola and his works (through 1952, as the date of the acknowledgments indicates).

Of the many books on Zola in English and those translated from French, here is a partial list of those which seem most helpful:

Barbusse, Henri, *Zola,* English translation by Mary B. and F. C. Green (New York: E. P. Dutton & Co., 1932).
Brown, Calvin Smith, *Repetition in Zola's Novels* (Athens: University of Georgia Press, 1952).
Brown, Donald Fowler, *The Influence of Émile Zola on the novelistic and critical Work of Emilia Pardo Bazan* (Urbana: University of Illinois Press, 1935).
Cézanne, Paul, *Letters,* edited by John Rewald (London: Cassirer, 1941).
Ellis, Havelock, *Affirmations* (London: Constable, 1915).
Friedman, Lee Max, *Zola and the Dreyfus Case* (Boston: Beacon, 1937).
Gosse, Edmund, *Questions at issue* (London, 1893). "The Limits of Realism in Fiction," pp. 137-54: mainly on Zola.
—— *French Profiles* (London: William Heinemann, 1913). "The Short Stories of Zola," pp. 129-52.
Josephson, Matthew, *Zola and his Time* (New York: Garden City, 1928).
Lukacs, George, *Studies in European Realism* (London, 1950). "The Zola Centenary," pp. 85-96.
Niess, Robert J., *Émile Zola's Letters to J. Van Santen Kolff* (St. Louis, 1940).

Patterson, J. G., *A Zola Dictionary*. The characters of the Rougon-Macquart novels of Émile Zola; with a biographical and critical introduction, synopses of the plots, bibliographical notes, map, genealogy, etc. (New York: Dutton, 1912.)

Rewald, John, *Paul Cézanne: a Biography* (New York: Simon & Schuster, 1948). English version of *Cézanne, sa vie, son oeuvre, son amitié pour Zola*, 1939.

―― *The Ordeal of Paul Cézanne* (London, 1950). A revised version of the above.

Root, Winthrop H., *German Criticism of Zola, 1875-93. With special reference to the Rougon-Macquart cycle and the experimental novel* (New York, 1931).

Rufener, Helen B. LaRue, *Biography of a War Novel, Zola's La Débâcle* (New York: King's Crown, 1946).

Sackville-West, Edward, *Inclinations* (London, 1949). "Zola's *La Débâcle*," pp. 199-204)

Sherard, Robert H., *Émile Zola, a Biographical and Critical Study* (London, 1893).

―― *Twenty years in Paris: being some recollections of literary life* (London, 1905).

Vizetelly, Ernest A., *With Zola in England* (London: Chatto, 1899).

―― *Émile Zola, Novelist and Reformer* (London & N. Y.: J. Lane, 1904).

Vizetelly, Henry, *Extracts principally from English Classics: showing that the legal suppression of M. Zola's novels would logically involve the bowdlerizing of some of the greatest of English literature* (London, 1888).

Wilson, Angus, *Émile Zola. An Introductory Study of His Novels* (New York: Morrow, 1952).

Acknowledgments

The illustrations contained in this book are reproductions of documents placed at our disposal by Émile Zola's family. We are pleased to express our gratitude to Doctor and Madame Jacques Zola for the very kind way in which they made our task easier in all respects. Thanks are also due M. Étienne Fasquelle, editor and friend of Zola, who died in 1952, and his son M. Charles Fasquelle, for their kind permission enabling us to reproduce these documents.

The photograph on page 88 is by Roger-Viollet. Acknowledgment is made to the following publishers for permission to quote passages: E. P. Dutton & Co. and J. M. Dent & Sons Ltd., *Zola*, by Henri Barbusse; Random House, *Nana*, translated by Ernest Boyd; Alfred A. Knopf, *Germinal*, translated by Havelock Ellis.

L'idée à priori, c'est la la poésie
(48)
à prendre très important 48
Raisonnement Expérimental historique de l'évolution de l'intelligence humaine (50)
Le point de départ de l'abstrait: les
voûtes subjectives, les math. puis la physiq
mathématique, puis les sciences expéri-
mentales (54).
Toute la théorie du roman expérimental (54)
L'expérimentateur est le juge d'instruction
de la nature (56)
L'hypothèse expéri. doit toujours être
fondée sur une observation antérieure (58)
La naissance de l'idée est le génie (59)
L'idée, c'est la graine, la méthode
c'est le sol (60)
La part du génie (62)
Le doute plus grand en biologie qu'en
physique (et dans le roman) (64)   (65)
La logique n'est pas l'expérien (Théâtre de Dumas